Emma Louisa Seeley

Belt and Spur

Stories of the Knights of the Middle Ages from the Old Chronicles

Emma Louisa Seeley

Belt and Spur

Stories of the Knights of the Middle Ages from the Old Chronicles

ISBN/EAN: 9783337294595

Printed in Europe, USA, Canada, Australia, Japan

Cover: Foto ©Thomas Meinert / pixelio.de

More available books at **www.hansebooks.com**

BELT AND SPUR

Stories of the Knights of the Middle Ages
from the Old Chronicles

With Sixteen Illuminations

> 'The heraudes left hir priking up and doun.
> Now ringen trompes loud and clarioun.
> Ther is no more to say, but est and west
> In goth the spores sadly in the rest;
> In goth the sharpe spore into the side.
> Ther see men who can juste, and who can ride.
> Ther shiveren shaftes upon sheldes thicke;
> He feleth thurgh the herte-spone the pricke.
> Up springen spores twenty foot on highte;
> Out gon the swerdes as the silver brighte.'
> — CHAUCER. *The Knightes Tale.*

FOURTH THOUSAND.

NEW YORK:
SCRIBNER AND WELFORD
MDCCCLXXXIV

All Rights Reserved.

CONTENTS.

		PAGE
I.	How Duke William and his Knights Landed in England	1
II.	The Battle of the Standard . . .	11
III.	King William the Lion	23
	How the young King Henry went away to the King of France, and how the Breton Barons rebelled against their King	23
	How King William raised an army and entered Northumberland	27
	How the Earl of Leicester came into England . .	34
	How King William of Scotland came again into England	38
	How King William was taken Prisoner . .	45
	How the tidings were brought to King Henry . .	49
IV.	Richard Cœur de Lion	54
	How Saladin took the Holy City, and how King Richard set out on a Crusade	54
	Of the taking of the City of Messina, and the coming of the Princess Berengaria	56
	Of the coming of Richard to Cyprus . . .	61
	Of the marriage of Richard and Berengaria, and the conquest of Cyprus	63

CONTENTS.

	PAGE
Of the coming of Richard to Acre, and the taking of the city	67
Of the departure of the King of France, and of the march of the army	70
Of the battle of Arsur, and the wonderful victory of the Christians	73
How William de Pratelles gave himself up for the King, and of the deeds of the Earl of Leicester	76
Of the rebuilding of Ascalon, and the discord among the Christians	79
How the Marquis Conrad was chosen King, and how he was slain by two young men	82
How King Richard took Darum and prepared to go up to Jerusalem	85
How Saladin came against Joppa, and of the admirable deeds of King Richard	90
How King Richard made peace with Saladin for three years, and set forth to return into his own land	94

V. FULK FITZWARINE 97

How Guarin of Metz won the love of Melette of the White Tower	97
How Fulk FitzWarine saved the life of Sir Joce de Dynan	100
How Fulk FitzWarine lost Whittington	103
How Fulk the younger angered Prince John, and how he, when he became king, refused Fulk justice	104
How Sir Fulk and his brothers hid in the woods, and the King appointed a hundred knights to take them	107
How Sir Fulk married Dame Maude de Caus, and slew a Knight named Sir Piers de Bruville	112
How Sir Fulk went to the Prince of Wales	116

		PAGE
Of Sir Audulf de Bracy and John de Rampaigne	.	119
How Sir Fulk and his brothers went over the sea to the King of France	.	122
How Sir Fulk took King John prisoner in the forest of Windsor	.	125
How Sir William Fitz Warine was rescued	.	129
How the King made peace with Sir Fulk and gave him back his lands, and how Sir Fulk died and was buried	.	131
VI. PRINCE EDWARD AT THE LAST CRUSADE	.	134
VII. THE SIEGE OF CAERLAVEROCK	.	145
VIII. THE BOLD DEEDS OF THE KNIGHTS OF SCOTLAND	.	152
IX. SEA-FIGHTS	.	165
X. THE BLACK PRINCE AT POITIERS	.	171
XI. THE JOUSTS OF ST. INGHELBERTH	.	181
Of the Enterprise of the three Knights	.	181
Of the First Day	.	186
Of the Second Day	.	193
Of the Third Day	.	195
Of the Fourth Day	.	197
XII. THE LAST DEEDS OF SIR HARRY HOTSPUR		202
Of Owen Glendower and the Earl Douglas	.	202
Of Henry Percy and Shrewsbury Field	.	206
XIII. KING HENRY THE FIFTH IN FRANCE	.	220
Of the Siege of Harfleur	.	220
How the King marched through the land	.	226

	PAGE
Of the Battle of Agincourt	229
Of the entry of the King into London	233
XIV. THE SIEGE OF ROUEN	238
XV. JACQUES DE LALAIN, KNIGHT OF THE FLEECE OF GOLD	260
How Sir Jacques challenged James Douglas	260
Of the Lists of Stirling	264
Of an English Squire who came to Bruges to fight with Sir Jacques	271
XVI. OF THE COMING OF QUEEN MARGARET OF ANJOU	277
XVII. THE ACT OF ARMS BETWEEN THE LORD SCALES AND THE BASTARD OF BURGUNDY	284

LIST OF ILLUSTRATIONS.

A GRANT OF LANDS FROM THE KING	*Frontispiece*
THE NORMAN KNIGHTS LANDING IN ENGLAND	8
PITCHING THE CAMP	32
RICHARD CŒUR DE LION IN BATTLE	56
RICHARD CŒUR DE LION AND THE EMPEROR OF CYPRUS	62
RIDING TO THE TOURNAMENT	98
WILLIAM FITZWARINE WOUNDED	128
SEA-FIGHT	168
HOW PEACE WAS PROCLAIMED	180
THE JOUSTS OF ST. INGHELBERTH	186
THE BATTLE OF SHREWSBURY	214
SAYING MASS	230
THE SIEGE OF ROUEN	242
THE DUKE OF BURGUNDY	272
TILTING WITH THE SPEAR	282
LORD SCALES AND THE BASTARD OF BURGUNDY	296

PREFACE.

THE following stories of battles and tournaments have been drawn from the pages of the old chronicles, and are told as the chronicler tells them; sometimes in an abridged and condensed form, but as far as possible, in the spirit and style of the original.

The story of Cœur de Lion's Crusade is taken from the 'Itinerary of Richard the First,' by Geoffrey Vinsauf. The deeds of the Scottish Knights in the reign of Edward the Third are related by Jean Le Bel, the chronicler whose work was so largely borrowed by Froissart. The Jousts of St. Inghelberth are described by Froissart himself. It is Henry the Fifth's chaplain who tells of his sovereign's achievements in France; and Chastelain, the Burgundian chronicler, who gives us the story of the tournaments at Stirling and at Bruges, in which Sir Jacques de Lalain bore a part.

Several of the other stories are taken from rhyming chronicles or historical poems. The account of the preparations for the conquest of England is drawn from the poem of the Norman, Robert Wace, whose father was an eye-witness of the events; and the story of William the Lion from Fantosme's 'Chronicle of Henry the Second.' The Battle of Poitiers is told as Chandos Herald relates it in his rhyming 'Life of the Black Prince;' and the Siege of Rouen is from the old English poem by John Page. The romance of Fulk FitzWarine, if less strictly history than the other tales, seems to have been founded on fact, and being probably nearly contemporary, gives at least a picture of the times.

The illustrations are mainly adapted from illuminated manuscripts in the British Museum.

E. L. S.

BELT AND SPUR.

CHAPTER I.

HOW DUKE WILLIAM AND HIS KNIGHTS LANDED IN ENGLAND.

Now Duke William was in his park at Rouen, and in his hands he held a bow ready strung, for he was going hunting, and many knights and squires with him. And behold, there came to the gate a messenger from England; and he went straight to the Duke and drew him aside, and told him secretly how King Edward's life had come to an end, and Harold had been made king in his stead. And when the Duke had heard the tidings, and understood all that was come to pass, those that looked upon him perceived that he was greatly enraged, for he forsook the chase, and went in silence, speaking no word to any man, clasping and unclasping his cloak, neither dared any man speak to him; but he crossed over the Seine in a boat, and went to his hall, and sat down on a bench; and he covered his face with his mantle, and leant down his head, and there he abode, turning about restlessly for one hour after another in gloomy thought. And none dared speak a word to him, but they spake to one another, saying, 'What ails the Duke? Why bears he such a mien?' Then there came in his seneschal riding from the park, and he went through the hall humming a song, and passed by the Duke; and there came many to him, asking him wherefore the Duke did so. And he answered them, 'You will hear the tidings soon, but be not in haste, for it is sure to leak out in time.' Then the Duke raised himself, and the seneschal came to him and said, 'Why conceal your tidings, sire, for if we know it not now, we shall hear it soon, and you will gain nothing by hiding it, nor lose by telling it; and though you may take great pains to hide it, all the town knows it? For they go about the city, little and great, saying that King Edward has passed away, and Harold is become king, and has received the kingdom.'

'That is it that troubles me,' said the Duke. 'I grieve because Edward is dead, and that Harold has done me wrong; for he has taken my kingdom who was bound to me by oath and promise.'

To these words answered FitzOsbern the bold, 'Sir, tarry not, but make ready with speed to avenge yourself on Harold, who has been disloyal to you; for if you lack not courage, there will be left no land to Harold. Summon all whom you may summon, cross the sea and seize his lands; for no brave man should begin a matter and not carry it on to the end.'

Then William sent messengers to Harold to call

upon him to keep the oath that he had sworn; but Harold replied in scorn that he would not marry his daughter, nor give up his land to him. And William sent to him his defiance; but Harold answered, that he feared him not, and he drove all the Normans out of the land, with their wives and children, for King Edward had given them lands and castles, but Harold chased them out of the country; neither would he let one remain. And at Christmas he took the crown, but it would have been well for himself and his land if he had not been crowned, since for the kingdom he perjured himself, and his reign lasted but a short space.

Then Duke William called together his barons, and told them all his will, and how Harold had wronged him, and that he would cross the sea and revenge himself; but without their aid he could not gather men enough, nor a large navy, therefore he would know of each one of them how many men and ships he would bring. And they prayed for leave to take counsel together, and the Duke granted their request. And their deliberations lasted long, for many complained that their burdens were heavy, and some said that they would bring ships and cross the sea with the Duke, and others said they would not go, for they were in debt and poor. Thus some would and some would not, and there was great contention between them.

Then FitzOsbern came to them and said, 'Wherefore dispute you, sirs? Ye should not fail your natural lord when he goes seeking honour. Ye owe him service for your fiefs, and where ye owe service ye should serve with all your power. Ask not delay, nor wait until he prays you; but go before, and offer him more than you can do. Let him not lament that his enterprise failed for your remissness.'

But they answered, 'Sir, we fear the sea, and we owe no service across the sea. Speak for us, we pray you, and answer in our stead. Say what you will, and we will abide by your words.'

'Will ye all leave yourselves to me?' he said. And each one answered, 'Yes. Let us go to the Duke, and you shall speak for us.'

And FitzOsbern turned himself about and went before them to the Duke, and spoke for them, and he said, 'Sir, no lord has such men as you have, and who will do so much for their lord's honour, and you ought to love and keep them well. For you they say they would be drowned in the sea or thrown into the fire. You may trust them well, for they have served you long and followed you at great cost. And if they have done well, they will do better; for they will pass the sea with you, and will double their service. For he who should bring twenty knights will gladly bring forty, and he who should serve you with thirty will bring sixty, and he from whom one hundred is due will willingly bring two hundred. And I, in loving loyalty, will bring in my lord's business sixty ships, well arrayed and laden with fighting men.'

But the barons marvelled at him, and murmured aloud at the words that he spake and the promises he made, for which they had given him no warrant. And many contradicted him, and there arose a noise and loud disturbance among them; for they feared that if they doubled their service it would become a custom, and be turned into a feudal right. And the noise and outcry became so great that a man could not hear what his fellow said. Then the Duke went aside, for the noise displeased him, and sent for the barons one by one, and spoke to each one of the greatness of the enterprise, and that if they would double their service, and do freely more than their due, it should be well for them, and that he would never make it a custom, nor require of them any service more than was the usage of the country, and such as their ancestors had paid to their lord. Then each one said he would do it, and he told how many ships he could bring, and the Duke had them all written down in brief. Bishop Odo, his brother, brought him forty ships, and the Bishop of Le Mans prepared thirty, with their mariners and pilots. And the Duke prayed his neighbours of Brittany, Anjou, and Maine, Ponthieu, and Boulogne, to aid him in this business; and he promised them lands if England were conquered, and rich gifts and large pay. Thus from all sides came soldiers to him.

Then he showed the matter to his lord the King of France, and he sought him at St. Germer, and found him there; and he said that if he would aid him, so that by his aid he won his right, he would hold England from him and serve him for it. But the King answered that he would not aid him, neither with his will should he pass the sea; for the French prayed him not to aid him, saying he was too strong already, and that if he let him add riches from over the sea to his lands of Normandy and all his good knights, there would never be peace. 'And when England shall be conquered,' said they, 'you will hear no more of his service. He pays little service now, but then it will be less. The more he has, the less he will do.'

So the Duke took leave of the King, and came away in a rage, saying, 'Sir, I go to do the best I can, and if God will that I gain my right you shall see me no more but for evil. And if I fail, and the English can defend themselves, my children shall inherit my lands, and thou shalt not conquer them. Living or dead, I fear no menace.'

Then he prayed to the Count of Flanders, as his friend and brother-in-law, to come and aid him; and the Count answered that he would know first how much he should have of England, and what part it would be. And to that the Duke answered that he would take counsel of his barons, and send him answer by letter. But when he came home he did a thing such as was never done before; for he took a little piece of parchment on which was neither writing nor letter, and he sealed it up, all blank as it was, and wrote outside that he would give him as much of England as was written within. And he gave it to a servant who had been long with him, and he brought it to the Count. And the Count broke the seal and spread open the parchment, and looked within; but when he found nothing, he showed it to the messenger. And the servant answered courteously,

'There is nothing within: nothing will you have.' I know not what the Count answered, but the servant took his leave.

Then the Duke sent to Rome clerks that were skilled in speech, and they told the Pope how Harold had sworn falsely, and that Duke William promised that if he conquered England he would hold it of St. Peter. And the Pope sent him a standard and a very precious ring, and underneath the stone there was, it is said, a hair of St. Peter's. And about that time there appeared a great star shining in the south with very long rays, such a star as is seen when a kingdom is about to have a new king. I have spoken with many men who saw it, and those who are cunning in the stars call it a comet.

Then the Duke called together carpenters and shipbuilders, and in all the ports of Normandy there was sawing of planks and carrying of wood, spreading of sails and setting up of masts, with great labour and industry. Thus all the summer long and through the month of August they made ready the fleet and assembled the men; for there was no knight in all the land, nor any good sergeant, nor archer, nor any peasant of good courage of age to fight whom the Duke did not summon to go with him to England.

When the ships were ready they were anchored in the Somme at St. Valery, and there came men to the Duke from many parts. There came Hamon, the Viscount of Thouars, a man of great power, and served by many; and Alan Fergant, who had great lands in Brittany; and Bertran FitzPelcit, and the

Lord of Dinan, and Raoul of Gael. And there came many a Breton from many a castle, and they of Brecheliant, of which the Bretons tell that there is a forest there, great and large, and much famed in Brittany, where the fountain of Berenton rises. There in times of great heat the hunters go, and, filling their horns with the water, pour it out on the rock, and then it rains all around the forest, I know not why. And there, too, fairies may be seen, if the Bretons speak the truth, and many other marvels; and it is wild with great plenty of large stags, but the peasant has forsaken it. There I went once seeking marvels, and I saw the forest and the land, and sought for marvels, but found none; a fool I went, and a fool returned.

And as the renown of the Duke went abroad there came to him soldiers one by one, or two by two, and the Duke kept them with him, and promised them much. And some asked for lands in England, and others pay and large gifts. But I will not write down what barons, knights, and soldiers, the Duke had in his company, but I have heard my father say (I remember it well, though I was but a boy) that there were seven hundred ships save four when they left St. Valery—ships, and boats, and little skiffs. But I found it written (I know not the truth) that there were three thousand ships carrying sails and masts.

And at St. Valery they tarried long for a favourable wind, and the barons grew weary with waiting; and they prayed those of the convent to bring out to the camp the shrine of St. Valery, and they came to

THE NORMAN KNIGHTS LANDING IN ENGLAND

it and prayed that they might cross the sea, and they offered money till all the holy body was covered with it, and the same day there sprang up a favourable wind. Then the Duke put a lantern on the mast of his ship, that the other ships might see it and keep their course near, and an ensign of gilded copper on the top, and at the head of the ship, which mariners call the prow, there was a child made of copper holding a bow and arrow, and he had his face toward England, and seemed about to shoot.

Thus the ships came to a port, and they all arrived together and anchored together, and they ran them together on the beach, and together they all disembarked. And it was near Hastings, and the ships lay side by side. And the good sailors, and sergeants, and esquires sprang out, and cast the anchors, and fastened the ships with ropes; and they brought out their shields and saddles, and led forth the horses. The archers were the first to come to land, every one with his bow bent and his quiver and arrows by his side, all shaven and dressed in short tunics, ready for battle, and of good courage; and they searched all the beach, but no armed man could they find. When they were issued forth, then came the knights in armour, with helmet laced and shield on neck, and together they came to the sand and mounted their war-horses; and they had their swords at their sides, and rode with lances raised. The barons had their standards and the knights their pennons. After them came the carpenters, with their axes in their hands and their tools hanging by their side. And when they came to the archers and to the knights they took counsel together, and brought wood from the ships and fastened it together with bolts and bars, and before the evening was well come they had made themselves a strong fort. And they lighted fires and cooked food, and the Duke and his barons and knights sat down to eat; and they all ate and drank plentifully, and rejoiced that they were come to land.

Now before the Duke was departed from the Somme there came to him a clerk learned in astronomy and necromancy, and he esteemed himself a seer, and foretold many things. And he had foretold to the Duke that he would pass the sea safely, and accomplish his design without fighting, for Harold would agree to hold the land of the Duke, and to become his liegeman, and that he would return in safety. He divined well about the passage, but about the battle he lied. And when the Duke had passed over, and was arrived safely, he remembered the seer, and asked for him. And one of his sailors answered that he was missing, and that it was said he had been drowned by the way. 'Then,' said the Duke, 'his knowledge was not great; he could not prophesy truly of me who knew not his own fate. If he knew the truth of everything, he would have foreseen his death. He is a fool who would fix the end of another and knows not his own time, but takes care for others and forgets himself.'

When the Duke came forth of his ship he fell on his hands to the ground, and there rose a great cry, for all said it was an evil sign; but he cried aloud,

'Lords, I have seized the land with my two hands, and will never yield it. All is ours.' Then a man ran to land and laid his hand upon a cottage, and took a handful of the thatch, and returned to the Duke. 'Sir,' said he, 'take seizin of the land; yours is the land without doubt.'

Then the Duke commanded the mariners to draw all the ships to land, and pierce holes in them, and break them to pieces, for they should never return by the way they had come.

CHAPTER II.

THE BATTLE OF THE STANDARD.

In the year of our Lord 1138, King Stephen being occupied in the south country, the King of the Scots gathered together an innumerable host, not of those only who owned his rule, but also not a few from the islands and from the Orkneys. With great ferocity and audacity he entered into the land of England, purposing either to subdue to his authority all the north of England, or to devastate it with fire and sword.

But the Archbishop Thurstan and Walter Espec roused the leaders beyond the Humber, and they, coming together, covenanted to resist him with force Therefore they assembled an army, few, indeed, in numbers, but strong in arms and valiant men, and, gathering together in a wide field near Allerton with the royal ensign, which is commonly called the Standard, waited to receive the enemy. For Thurstan, the archbishop, had sent his edict throughout his whole diocese, commanding that all who could go to war should gather hastily to the leaders to defend the Church of Christ against the barbarian host, and that from every parish they should come, led by the priests with the cross and the holy ensigns. In the southern army among the leaders there was William, Earl of Albemarle, young but valiant, and well exercised in arms, having with him many soldiers, and being not less excellent in military astuteness than in courage. And there was Walter de Ghent, in extreme old age, a gentle and good man, himself leading his Flemings and Normans, and encouraging the people much by his wisdom and the weight of his words. Neither was Gilbert de Lacy slow to come; and he, having lived long in exile in King Henry's time, had grown used to toil and hardship, and in this time of necessity remained unmoved. And Robert de Bruce, though he was in friendship with the King of the Scots, failed not the people in this extremity, but came to this place with his young son Adam and a company of brave youths. And so fervently were all men moved to resist the Scots that there came Roger de Mowbray, who was but a lad, to be with the army, though it would have been more proper for him at his age to have remained at home. And with him assembled all the men of his lands with such zeal and devotion that neither in wisdom, courage, nor numbers, did they seem inferior to the rest, so that the little age of their lord seemed no loss to any of the army.

And there was Walter Espec, an old man and full of days, acute in mind, prudent in counsel, modest in peace, wary in war, ever loyal to the King and faithful to his friends. He was a man of great stature, with mighty limbs and thick black hair and beard, and a voice like a trumpet, and he was great and ready in speech. He came of noble race, and was noble in deeds of Christian piety.

Then he, being held in honour by the whole army on account of his age and wisdom, ascending the machine which was constructed round the royal ensign, encouraged the dejected and animated the eager. 'Hear me, oh, brave men!' he said, 'for I have lived long and seen many wars and changes of time. I see many of you wavering and hesitating, fearing greatly that our little company will be swallowed up by the great host of the Scots; but victory depends not on multitudes, but on strength and a good cause. Therefore, considering what a cause, what a necessity brings us here to fight against such enemies, I stand intrepid, as secure of victory as of battle. Why should we despair of victory when victory has, as it were, been given in fief to our race by the Highest? Did not our ancestors, in small numbers, invade a large part of Gaul, erasing even the name? Did not our fathers and we, in short space, subdue this island, which cost the victorious Julius many years of hard fighting? We have seen with our own eyes the King of France and all his army turn their backs, and the greatest leaders of his kingdom led captive. Who subdued Apulia, Sicily, and Calabria? Did not both the emperors flee before the Normans almost on the same day and hour, one fighting against the father and the other against the son? And who would not rather laugh than fear at having to fight with half-naked Scots? These are they who yielded without resistance when William, conqueror of English and

Scots, advanced to Abernethy? What are their spears that they should terrify us so greatly? Of fragile wood and blunt iron, they break in piercing, and are scarce strong enough for one thrust. Save for a stick, the Scots are unarmed. And shall we fear numbers? The greater the numbers the greater the glory of conquest. And for what a cause do we fight! None will deny us the right of fighting for our country, for our wives and children, and for our Church in such extreme peril. Remember what befell beyond the Tyne, and hope for nothing better if the Scots conquer. I will not speak of the slaughter and rapine, such as no history related of the cruellest tyrants. No order, no age, no sex, were spared. Noble boys and girls were carried away captive, and little children borne on the points of spears by the men of Galloway, churches entered and polluted. You have to fight not with men, but with beasts, who know no humanity nor piety, whom Heaven abhors and the earth abominates, and who would have been swallowed up by the earth, or struck down by lightning, or drowned in the sea, but that they are reserved for you to conquer. Then let us join battle with assured minds, for ours is the just cause; our hands are stronger, necessity, glory urge us, Divine aid will be ours, and all the heavenly host will fight for us.' Then he turned him to the Earl of Albemarle, and taking him by the hand, 'I swear,' said he, 'this day to conquer the Scots, or fall by the hands of the Scots.'

And all the leaders bound themselves by a like

vow. And that all hope of flight should be entirely taken away, they dismounted to fight on foot, and all the horses were removed to a distance, for they desired either to conquer or die.

In the meanwhile the King of the Scots, having assembled his earls and the chief leaders of his kingdom, began to hold counsel with them; and some advised that armed men and bowmen should go before the army, so that armed men might be opposed to armed men, soldiers to soldiers, and bowmen to bowmen. But to that the men of Galloway replied, that it was their right to hold the front rank and first attack the enemy, animating the rest of the host by their valour. But others thought it perilous thus to make the first attack with unarmed men, for if not sustaining the force of the battle, the first line should take to flight, the hearts of the strong would melt. Nevertheless the men of Galloway demanded that their right should be conceded to them. 'What fearest thou, O King? and why art thou so greatly terrified at those coats of mail? Our sides are iron, our breasts brass, our minds are free from fear, and our feet have never known flight, nor our backs a wound. We bore away the victory from the armed men at Cliderhou, and this day will we overthrow the spearmen.'

But perceiving that the King leaned to the counsel of the soldiers, Malis, Earl of Strathearn, cried out in anger, 'Wilt thou, O King, yield to the will of the Gauls? but I swear that no man in armour shall this day precede me in the battle.' At which words the young Alan de Percy, a strong man and well proved in military matters, restraining his anger with difficulty, turned him to the Earl and said, 'Thou hast spoken words this day which thou wilt not be able to make good.' Then the King, bidding them both be silent, lest a tumult should have arisen from the altercation, yielded to the will of the men of Galloway.

The second line being given to the King's son, he set the soldiers and bowmen in array with great skill, the Cumbrians and men of Teviotdale being joined with them. And the youth was handsome in person and proper in demeanour, of so great humility that he seemed inferior to all, of so great authority that he was feared by all, gentle and affable, so that he was beloved by all; decorous in manners, sober in speech, honest in all things, devout, apt to speak, benevolent to the poor, firm against evil-doers, a monk among kings and a king among monks. He was also of such valour that there was none like him in attack or in sustaining an attack, swift in pursuit, fierce in repelling, slow in flight. There was joined with him Eustace FitzJohn, one of the great leaders of England who had been familiar with the late King Henry, a man of great prudence and counsel in secular matters, who had forsaken the king of the English because an accusation having been brought against him concerning some castles that Henry had given him he was compelled to restore them, on which account he joined the enemy to take his revenge.

In the third line were the men of Lothian and the Isles, and the Highlanders. The King retained in his own line the Scots and the men of Moray, and English and French knights to guard his person. Such was the array of the northern army.

The little company of the southerners was ordered with great skill in one body. For, the most valiant men-at-arms being placed in front, there were mixed with them lancers and bowmen, who, protected by the armed men, might securely and fiercely meet the enemy's attack; and the elder leaders assembled round the standard, that they might thence command the army. Then shields were joined to shield side to side, lances with pennons unfurled were raised, the coats-of-mail glittered in the sun, and the priests, clad in their sacred white garments, went round the army with crosses and relics of saints, strengthening and animating the men with their exhortations.

Then Robert de Bruce, a man of great age and of great deeds, grave in manners and of rare speech, whose words were with weight, who, while he was by oath one of the King of England's men, had in youth joined the King of the Scots, and been admitted to familiar friendship with him,—he, therefore, a man of military experience and well known in such matters, seeing the peril which hung over the King, moved by his ancient friendship, went, with the leave of the confederate leaders, to the King, that he might dissuade him from war, or persuade him to wage it more lawfully. When, therefore, he was come to the King, he spake thus, saying, 'I come, O King, to give thee good counsel, useful to thy kingdom and to thy posterity; for he is wise who looks not only to the

beginning, but to the results of deeds. Against whom
dost thou fight this day? Is it not against the
English and the Normans? And have they not often
aided thee? Nay, wilt thou be safe from the Scots
without their aid? With whose aid did thy brother
Duncan, son of Donald, overcome his enemies?
Who restored thy brother Edgar to his kingdom?
Thou thyself obtainedst the portion of land which
thy dying brother left thee from thy brother Alexander through our terror. And remember how but
the year past there came to thy aid against thine
enemy Malcolm, gladly and swiftly, Walter Espec,
and other English leaders, and overcame him and
delivered him into thine hand; and, in truth, the Scots
hate us because we have served and aided thee. For-
bear then, O King, for thine own sake, and for thy
kingdom's sake, and, above all, for the sake of thy
noble young son. Why dost thou join in the sins of
wicked men, at whose hands will be required the
slaughter of babes and women, and the sacrilege of
holy things; against whom the blood, not of one
Abel, but of innumerable innocent victims, cries from
the ground? Declare thou that these deeds are done
against thy will. For there is opposed to thee no
contemptible army, but one as much superior to thine
in arms and good soldiers as it is inferior to thine in
numbers. And thou knowest, O King, the courage
of despair. If thou conquer, we die certainly: we, and
our little ones, and our wives; and our priests will be
murdered at the altar. But we are resolved to conquer or to die gloriously; and none of us doubts of

victory. Therefore, I mourn, I weep, because for my dear lord, my friend, my old companion, in whose friendship I have grown old, whose generous munificence I have known, with whom I played in boyhood, and in whose dangers I have shared, there remains nothing but death or a shameful flight.'

He ceased, his voice choked with tears and grief; and the King was moved to tears and instantly would have made peace. But William, the King's nephew, a man strong of will and bent on war, came between them, and with great fury accusing Robert of treason, moved the King from his purpose. Robert, therefore, delaying no longer, according to the manner of his country, renounced the faith by which he was bound to the King, and returned to his men—not without grief.

Then, straightway, the northern army advanced with lances raised, and with the shrill blast of clarion and trumpets and the clash of arms, the heavens and the earth trembled, and mountain and hill resounded.

In the meantime, Radulph, Bishop of the Orkneys, whom Archbishop Thurstan had sent to them, standing on a high place, gave absolution to the people, who, beating their breasts and lifting up their hands, prayed to Heaven for aid; and absolution being pronounced, the Bishop blessed them solemnly. And the people cried aloud, 'Amen! amen!'

Then the men of Galloway, uttering after their manner yells and horrible cries, ran upon the southern army with such fury that they forced the spearmen to give way; but they, being supported by the soldiers, soon recovered their courage, and the lances of the Scots proving of delusive brittleness, they drew their swords and sought to fight hand to hand. But the southerners poured upon them a dense rain of arrows, and assailed them with such a ceaseless shower of missiles in their breasts and faces, that they retarded their attack. Nevertheless, the men of Galloway, bristling with arrows as the hedgehog with its spines, brandishing their swords, fell in blind fury upon their enemies, striking vain blows upon the empty air. Then, suddenly overcome by a panic of fear, they dissolved into flight; when the King's noble young son, coming up with his company, with lion-like fury broke the southern lines like cobweb, and cutting down all who opposed, swept beyond the royal standard, supposing himself to be followed by the rest of the army, and that he might make it impossible for the enemy to escape, he attacked the place where the horses were stationed, dispersed them and drove them away for a space of two miles. Terrified by the force of this attack, the unarmed men began to give way; but a certain wise man, holding up the head of a man that had been slain, cried out that the King was slain; and thus they were encouraged and stood firm.

Then the men of Galloway, being unable to stand longer before the shower of arrows and the swords of the soldiers, turned to flee, two of their leaders, Ulric and Donald, being slain. And the men of Lothian, scarce waiting for the first attack, melted away. Thereupon the King and the leaders, leaping from their horses, advanced upon the enemy. But the Scots, panic-struck at the flight of the others, began to drop away from the royal troop, until, in a short time, there were but few left round the King. Then the army of the English advanced upon them, and the King himself, and all his men, would have been taken or slain, if his soldiers, having vainly implored him to flee, had not lifted him upon his horse and compelled him to retire. And those who were fleeing, seeing the royal ensign, which being a dragon was easily recognised, and perceiving that the King had not fallen, returned to him and formed a body to oppose those who were pursuing.

In the meantime, that flower of youth and glory of chivalry—the King's son—looking behind him, saw himself with but few men in the midst of the enemy. Then, turning him to one of his companions, he said, smiling, 'We have done what we could, and certainly we have overcome as many as ourselves, and it is a sign of a great mind not to be broken in adverse fortune, and when we cannot overcome by strength to do so by prudence. Therefore, let us divide one from another, and join ourselves to the enemy, as if we were pursuing with them, that so we may pass them by, and get as soon as possible to my father, whom I see yielding to necessity.' This said, spurring his horse he passed through the midst of his enemies, and having issued beyond, slackened his horse's speed. Then he, with his knights, throwing away their heavy armour, came to a poor cottage, and, calling out the peasant, he took off his princely chain, and casting it at the man's feet, said, 'Take what is a burden to me, but may help you in your need.'

And the King, having put a distance between himself and his enemies, gathered a company and set them again in array, hoping to capture some who were pursuing, that thus he might deter others from attacking ; and he came to Carlisle, and there, being in safety himself, he awaited his son in great fear for two days, but the third day he received him safe and sound.

And the English leaders pursuing far, took prisoners and killed great numbers, both of the Scots and the men of Galloway ; and all the English leaders returned safe and uninjured, and gathering round Walter Espec, whom they venerated as their captain and father, gave great thanks to Almighty God for such an unhoped-for victory.

CHAPTER III.

KING WILLIAM THE LION.

How the young King Henry went away to the King of France, and how the Breton barons rebelled against their King.

THE King of England called his barons together, and caused his son to be crowned king, and made the King of Albany and all his barons do homage to him, saying,—'God curse all who would part you, or break the love between you. Stand by my son, and aid him against all the world, saving my seigniory.'

But between him and his son there grew up a deadly hatred, which cost many a gentle knight his life, for when he could not have his will, because of his father, he went away secretly, and passed over the Loire, and would tarry neither for meat and drink till he came to St. Denis, and recounted all to the King of France. Then there was held a great assembly, and Philip of Flanders and Matthew of Boulogne were summoned; and the Count of Flanders encouraged the King to go to war with the King of England. And Count Thibault rose from his seat and said, 'Gentle King of St. Denis, I am your liegeman by faith and homage, and am ready to serve you for forty days; and I will do to King Henry such damage as shall not be restored all his life, nor shall he rest until he have given back his heritage to the young King, his son.'

And the King and his barons agreed, and they sent messengers to defy King Henry; and the host of France was summoned in the month of April, at Easter. King Henry rode against them with ten thousand Brabançons, and many a gentle knight of Anjou and Gascony.

The host of France that Louis led was great, for the son took great pains to destroy his father, and trusted to lead him vanquished and a prisoner to St. Denis; but the King, his father, vowed that he should see many a banner, and many a costly horse, and gaily painted shield, and many a bold joust fought out, ere he would yield himself recreant and conquered. But the lord of England was heavy at heart, because his son, whom he nourished in childhood, made war upon him; yet would he rather die than give his son the power while he could wield sword or lance. And he went against Louis, the mighty King of France, and Count Philip, and his brother, the valiant knight Matthew. And God aided the father that day, and Count Matthew of Boulogne received a mortal wound, and the blood ran down to his gilt spurs, and his brother sorrowed greatly, and swore that his wrath against King Henry should never be appeased.

And with the French and Flemings opposed to King Henry rode the Earl of Leicester and all his three sons, and the lord of Tancarville at the head of a hundred knights. But, by my troth, I know not why his vassals demeaned them so towards him, for he was the most honourable and victorious king that had ever reigned in any land since the time of Moses, excepting only the King Charles, with Oliver and Roland, and the twelve companions.

Then rode Count Philip through the land of Normandy, wasting it by wood and plain; and the barons of Brittany submitted to the young King's command, which when King Henry heard, he was much grieved. 'Lords,' said he to his knights, 'nothing in my life has vexed me so sore; I am mad with rage that the barons of Brittany should have gone against me, and joined those who hate me to the death, King Louis of France and my eldest son, who would disinherit me. I am not yet so old that I should lose my lands because of my great age. But Raoul of Fougeres has rebelled against me, and Earl Hugh of Chester has joined with him; but for no cost of gold will I fail to follow them to their fortresses, and against such enemies craft is better than war.'

Then his knights hastened, and leaving the palace seized their arms, clad themselves in hauberks and breastplates, and laced on their helmets, and took up their Viennese shields. And King Henry, as he rode out of the town at the head of his knights in array, cried, 'It will be evil for the traitors to meet us in the fields!' Then his men rode to Dol in Brittany.

And the men in the castle looked out, and saw William de Humet coming with the banner, and the Brabançons behind; and they went to Sir Raoul and cried, 'See the host of Normandy which is coming upon us! Normans are good conquerors, as we hear in every tale. The young king has betrayed us. How can we defend ourselves?'

And Sir Raoul replied, 'He who has good counsel let him speak. But let us not be dishonoured, nor the land ravaged. The castle is not strong, let us issue forth and assail them.' So they came out to the plain and joined battle with William de Humet and his company. There was no knight of name who did not break a lance, but each one who would joust found his match, and the Breton barons were driven back into their fortresses. No mangonel nor engine for stones would have helped them, but the war which they had begun cost them dear. For a messenger on a black horse rode to King Henry at Rouen, and when he heard of the discomfiture of his enemies he came with haste to Dol. And his coming sent fear into his enemies, and for lack of victual they rendered them up into his power.

'My lords,' said King Henry, 'my son takes rent by force from all my fiefs, and it does not seem right to me that it should be paid to him. They of Flanders are against me. Aid me, lords, to guard my rights. Earl Hugh of Chester take along with you. As for Raoul of Fougeres, I let him go free

in his lands, if he will give me his faith; but if he
ever rebel against me again he shall hold in Brittany
neither fief nor heritage. Now, lords, to horse; my
son is in battle array. Let us go and pay him his
rent with our swords and sharp darts.' And his
knights were glad, and rejoiced at his words, but
the Earl of Chester mourned, fearing never to be
loosed from prison.

How King William raised an army, and entered Northumberland.

Then King Louis wrote a letter, and sealed it
with a ring, and called before him the messengers
of the young king; and they having received the
letter, traversed the salt sea, passed forests and plains,
and came to Scotland; and finding the King, presented the writing to him, on the part of the young
King Henry; and in the letter was written,—

'To the King of Scotland, William the Good, King
Henry the younger sends you love, and bids you remember
him who is your lord. I marvel much that so rich a king,
and a man of thy valour, with such force of men, gives me
no aid in warring against my father. I will give thee the
lands that thy ancestors held, the lands beyond Tyne. I
know no better under the heavens; and Carlisle will I
give, that none may be able to oppose thee in Westmoreland, if thou wilt aid me against those who hold my lands.'

Then the King of Scotland had great searchings
of heart when he heard how the young king claimed
his homage against all people, and how he would
give him the lands that all the kings of Scotland had

held, for he owed homage to the old king, the father, also, and true allegiance; neither were it right that he should destroy his land.

Then he called together his parliament, and told them of the letter of the young king, and he said, 'I will send messengers to the father in Normandy, that he give me back the part of my inheritance, Northumberland, which he withholds from me; and if he refuse to give it me, I owe him no longer either faith or friendship.'

To that answered the Earl Duncan, 'The old king is reasonable, seek not occasion to do him outrage. Fair words are better than menaces. He who holds not so, seeks his own death and confusion. If he give you your rights you will serve him as his liegeman.'

Thus spake Earl Duncan wisely, and the counsel pleased the King and his barons; and the messengers departed, and spurred their horses, and rode with slack reins over the great paved roads. And they came to Normandy, and found the old King Henry, and gave him the letters of the King of Scotland. And Friar William Dolepene said to the King, 'I am a messenger from the King of Scotland, your kinsman, who should be dear to you. Within a month he will come to you with a thousand armed knights, and thirty thousand unarmed men, against your enemies; neither will he ask of you a penny, so you will grant him his rights, and chiefly Northumberland; but if you will not, but will disinherit him, he gives you back your homage.'

When the King heard this demand, he made answer to the messenger, 'Say to the King of Scotland I fear nothing from the war that I have with my son, neither do I fear the King of France and his men, nor the Count of Flanders. I will make them lament the war they have begun. But say to his brother David, my kinsman, that he come to me with all the men he has, and I will give him lands, and all that he desires.'

So the messengers departed from Normandy, and traversed England, and came into Albany; and there was none that harmed them from Dover to Orkney, but soon will there be such tales of war as shall make many weep.

'God save thee, sir King of Scotland! I am returned from the King of England. Much he marvels at you. He held you for a wise man, and no child in age, and you demand his land as your inheritance, as if he were a bird in a cage. He is no fugitive nor outlaw, but the King of England; nor will he give you increase of land.'

And when the hot-blooded young knights heard that, they swore great oaths, and said, 'If you do not make war on this king, who shames you so, you are not worthy to hold land nor lordship, but should serve the son of Matilda.'

But there was not there Ingelram, the Bishop, neither did Earl Waltheof counsel war — he knew well it was folly; but the King, led away by foolish men, answered him in anger, 'Your cowardice will not prevent the war. You have treasure enough

—defend your lands; but if you will not give aid, you shall not have of the spoil the value of a clove of garlic.' But the Earl answered, 'I am your liegeman, and so were my kinsmen. But trust not in strangers, for if you prosper they will gain; but if you lose they cannot suffer. Nevertheless, I will not fail you while I live.'

Then the King sent messengers to Flanders to the young King Henry, to promise him aid, and to pray him to send to him Flemings with ships. And they departed and came to Berwick, and entered into barges, and hoisted their sails, and went on the high sea; for they cared not to coast along England, for those who were friends were now become their mortal enemies. And they found their lord with King Louis of France and Count Philip. And Count Philip gave counsel and said, 'Pledge your faith to the King of Scotland, and bid him make war on your enemies, and waste their land with fire and destroy it utterly. Within fifteen days we will give him aid from Flanders.' And King Louis agreed, and the messengers returned to their own land.

And every man encouraged his neighbour, and said, 'Let us go and take the Castle of Wark in England.' And all boasted of the victory that was promised them. And the King of Scotland assembled his army, and there came men from Ross and Moray, and the Earl of Angus came with three thousand Scots; and there were assembled such a multitude of naked men as had not been seen for many ages.

So King William came to Wark in England, which was a castle in the marches, and he sent to the constable to know if he would hold it or yield it up. Now the constable was Roger de Stuteville, no lover of treason, but he saw that his force was not enough to stand against the host of Scotland, and he lamented with tears the fallen power of his King. Then, in his wisdom, he came before the King of Scotland, and prayed for forty days' space, that he might send sealed letters across sea or go himself and tell his lord that all his people were given up to destruction. And King William, seeing his great sadness, granted his request. And the wise knight went himself to England and prayed for succour, and within the term appointed he led back such a host that he gave full leave to the King of Scotland to attack him.

So the King William said to his knights, 'Let us go through Northumberland; there is none to oppose us, for the Bishop of Durham tells me by letters that he wishes to be at peace. Let us go to Alnwick, and if William de Vesci will yield up his father's castle I will let him go without loss of limb.' So they came to Alnwick, but William de Vesci being prepared to defend it, they made no long stay, but departed and came to Warkworth. Roger Fitz-Richard had it in ward, but it was weak, and he could not hold it. But he was Lord of New Castle on Tyne, and would make no peace with the King of Scotland. And the King came against him with his armed men and his naked tribes; but the barons loved their lord, and held it

PITCHING THE CAMP

better to die or lose their heritage than suffer shame. Then the King William saw well that he could not conquer New Castle by storm; but his counsellors said, 'Be not downcast, but let the host be ready early in the morning, and let us go to Carlisle and conquer it. When Robert de Vaux sees so many shields and Poitevin helmets he will wish himself a bishop.' But King William answered, 'May I be for ever put to shame if I make terms with Odonel, for as long as Castle Prudhoe stands we shall never have peace in Scotland.' And he bade them pitch his tents before it; but his barons refused to aid him, saying, 'Carlisle is the hardest to secure of all your rights. Go, then, and conquer the chief place; lay siege to it, and make your host swear not to depart from it until it has been set on fire and the walls pulled down with pickaxes and Robert de Vaux hanging on a high gallows. He cannot long resist you.' And to this counsel the King agreed.

So on the morrow, when day appeared, the trumpets sounded, and King William and all his barons and his host set out on their march. Now the King of Scotland understood how to make war on his enemies and to do them hurt and damage, but he turned too much to new counsels, and cherished strangers, holding them dear, but his own people he loved not.

And having set his men in array, he assaulted the walls. Great was the noise of clanging iron and clashing steel; scarce a helmet or hauberk was left whole. That day those within showed themselves knights, and left many strewed round the walls with no leisure to rise. But they must aid themselves and hold their barbican, and fight for it; and they had no need of cowards, for the assault at the gates was fierce.

Then there came in haste to the King a messenger—a canon he was, and knew the language; and the King was in his pavilion, and with him his chamberlains and his friends, while the warriors stood around. And he told them how he had seen armed men and knights who were prepared to assail him before the sun rose. 'And De Lucy will be with them before midnight, and many come with him. Listen to good counsel, and go for safety to Roxburgh, for if you delay, evil will be the song that is sung of you.' But the King answered in anger, swearing by St. Andrew, 'We are safe enough here, and will not refuse to give battle, for a brave man must fight for his rights. My ancestors held this land, and I will not yield a foot of it while I live.'

But his men gave him better counsel, and prayed him to leave the siege. And he yielded, and none drew rein till they came to Roxburgh. And they rode by night as those in haste ere any assault had been made, or they had suffered damage.

How the Earl of Leicester came into England.

Thus Sir Richard de Lucy, with the English host, rode secure through the wasted and ruined country, for whereas Northumberland had been fruitful and its people honoured, now there was great famine — all was destroyed. And he cursed the war, and thought in his heart that he would have revenge. But there came to him a messenger bearing tidings that the Earl of Leicester was come into the land, having joined with the Flemings and the French to subdue England.

Then Sir Richard de Lucy sought to make peace with the King of Scotland, but there was gone out from his host Sir Humphrey de Bohun and the barons of Northumberland, and had set on fire Berwick and all the lands around. But Sir Richard, in his wisdom, made a truce with the King of Scotland for Northumberland until the summer.

Now Earl Robert of Leicester was come into Suffolk and many Flemish gentlemen with him, and all gave way before him until he came to Dunwich. And Earl Hugh Bigod sent messengers to the men of Dunwich that they should join the Earl, but they would not assent. Then the Earl of Leicester swore he would not leave a man of them alive, and set up the gallows to put them in fear, and armed his men in haste to assail the town. But the burghers ran to their defences, and each one knew his business, shooting with bows or throwing darts, and the maidens and women carried stones to throw from the palisades. So the men of Dunwich defended themselves, and showed themselves such brave men that Earl Robert had to leave with shame.

Then at dawn of day he said to his constables,

'Bid the men mount their horses, for I will go to Norwich.' As for those who would know the truth how Norwich was taken, I was not in the country when it was besieged; but a traitor of Lorraine betrayed it, and so it was taken by surprise. There is no country worth Norfolk from here to Montpellier, no better knights nor merrier dames, except the city of London, to which there is no peer. Ah, gentle King of England, what love you owe to London and her barons! for they never failed their rightful lord, but were always first in his business. But there came messengers enough from Flanders across the sea, promising them great honours. And your son sent them letters promising to love and cherish them all the days of his life, and give them great things if they would give him aid; but they would not.

The Earl of Leicester went on wasting the land of Norfolk, having with him Flemings by hundreds and thousands; and Earl Hugh Bigod aiding him in everything. Then the Earl Ferrars sent him letters, bidding him ride through the land. 'The King of Scotland, and David his brother, and Sir Roger de Mowbray, will go to war to succour you. If you can ride to Leicester before Easter, you will be able to go as far as the Tower of London.'

And the Earl asked counsel of his knights; and his wife answered him, 'Will you fear to ride because of Humphrey de Bohun and the Earl of Arundel? The English are good boasters, but they know not how to fight; they are better at drinking and guzzling. The Earl of Gloucester is to be feared; but he has your sister to wife, and for all the wealth of France would commit no outrage on you.'

'Dame,' said the Earl, 'I must take your counsel for the love I bear you.' And Sir Hugh du Chastel gave like counsel. And the Flemings were glad, and cried aloud, 'We came not into this land to sojourn, but to destroy the old King Henry, and get his wool!' For most of them were weavers and not knights, and came to get spoil: and the lands of St. Edmund's were rich.

The Earl of Leicester was a man of great power, but too young and childish was the courage that made him go through England robbing and destroying, with his wife armed and bearing shield and lance. But the lands of St. Edmund's had knights of great power, who armed in haste. There was Walter Fitz-Robert, and the Earl of Arundel, and Sir Humphrey de Bohun. And the Earl of Leicester saw the armed men approaching, and cried to Sir Hugh du Chastel, 'Let us go no further, but give battle here; see the helmets and the hauberks shining in the sun. Bear yourselves as knights, and woe be to the man who flees first!'

Then was Walter Fitz-Robert the first to attack, and fell upon the Flemings fiercely; but they were more than he by hundreds and by thousands, and they drove him back with his men. And he cried to the Earl for aid, and he came on fiercely with a great oath; and Roger Bigod also, nor was Hugh de Cressi wanting. Robert Fitz-Bernard made great slaughter of the strangers, and they gathered little wool that day; but the crows and buzzards came down upon their dead bodies. Better would have been for them to have stayed in Flanders.

The Earl of Leicester and Sir Hugh du Chastel were helpless in the crowd. My lady the Countess met with a ditch, in which she was nearly drowned; and lost her rings in the mud. They will never be found again, I trow. She desired drowning rather than life; but Simon de Vahille raised her up, saying, 'Lady, come with me; so goes the fortune of war— now gaining, and now losing!' And Earl Robert was dismayed, and turned pale when he saw his wife taken, and his companions killed by hundreds and by thousands. And Sir Humphrey de Bohun and the Earl of Arundel took him and Hugh du Chastel, and the villagers of the country came destroying the Flemings with forks and flails; as the knights knocked them down, the peasants slew them, throwing them into the ditches by forties and fifties, and hundreds and thousands.

Thus Earl Robert was discomfited, and England made more secure; but the Flemings' lot was hard.

How King William of Scotland came again into England.

Then, in May, when the grass was growing green, came David of Scotland into the land, a gentle knight, who hurt not priest, nor robbed church nor abbey; but the King of Scotland had given him Lennox and Huntingdon to be his man, to fight against King Henry. And he came with helmets and hauberks, and many fine shields; and the Earl of Leicester's men sent to him and prayed him to come to their castle. And he came, and won him honour and renown.

After Easter, the King of Scotland returned to waste Northumberland, and Roger de Stuteville had strengthened Wark; so the King by night arrayed many knights and sent them to Bamborough Castle, and they did marvellous damage, for the people were asleep in their beds. And they came to the town of Belford and assailed it, and scattered themselves over the country, seizing the sheep and burning the towns, and binding and dragging away the peasants, while the women fled miserably to the minster. And they returned to Berwick with great spoil of cattle and horses, fine cows and sheep and lambs, and cloth and jewels.

So the King summoned all the knights of his land, for he would lay siege to Wark; because he had with him Flemings and archers, and good machines for throwing stones, and slingers and cross-bowmen. But Roger was not dismayed, and he had more than twenty knights with him, the best that ever lord had, and he had strengthened his house.

Then, on a Monday morning, the Flemings began the assault, and with marvellous boldness came within the ditches, and they fought hand to hand, all mingled together; shields and bucklers breaking, pennons waving, the wounded Flemings turning back from the portcullis, or borne away never to cry 'Arras!' again. The assault lasted long, and Roger encouraged his men and exhorted them, saying, 'Shoot not your arrows too often, for they are without, and rich in arms; but we are shut up here, so spare your arms, but when you see the time, defend yourselves like knights!'

Then the King, seeing that nothing was gained, bade them bring near the great engine for casting stones to break down the gate. But, behold the first stone that was cast fell backwards, and brought to the ground one of their own knights, that, but for his armour, he would never have returned home. Then the King, full of rage and fury, would have set fire to the castle, but the wind was contrary; so, having watched all night, at dawn of day he made his earls and barons assemble, and said, 'Gentle knights, let us leave this siege, for we can do nothing, and have gained great loss; burn down your huts and fold up your tents, and let all the host return to Roxburgh.'

And when Sir Roger heard the noise of their departure, and saw them going away towards Roxburgh, he said to his men, 'Rail not at them, nor cry, nor shout; but let us praise God our Father, that He has delivered our lives from such a proud host.' So there were no reproaches, nor insults, but songs and glad rejoicings; for none were slain or wounded within the castle. But the King was sore at heart, and swore a great oath that he would not give up the war, though he should lose his kingdom.

Then came Roger de Mowbray to the King, having left his castles in the care of his two eldest sons, and prayed the King to come against royal

Carlisle, and with him Sir Adam de Port, and they were the best knights in the world. And the King was glad, and went with all his host against fair Carlisle, the strong city. And they came where they could see it in its beauty, with the walls and turrets shining in the sun. And there was trembling in the city; but Robert de Vaux encouraged them.

And the King sent Roger, and Adam, and Walter de Berkeley to the town to Sir Robert de Vaux, saying, 'Yield up to me the castle, for there is none to succour thee; and if thou wilt not thou shalt lose thy head, and thy children shall die, and all thy friends and kinsmen will I exile.' So they came to Sir Robert, and he leant on a battlement, clad in a hauberk with a sharp sword in his hand; and the messengers summoned him to give up the castle to the King of Scotland as the rightful lord. But Sir Robert answered, 'We care not for threats nor promises; but let the King go to King Henry and complain that I hold the castle against him, and if my lord is angry with me, send me his message. Or give me respite till I cross the sea and tell my lord King Henry. If he will not, I will die here, before I surrender my lord's castle.'

So the messengers returned and told the King; and he went away and came to Appleby, where there was no guard, and took it; for the constable Gospatrick, son of Horm, an old Englishman, soon cried mercy. At that the King was much rejoiced, and swore great threats against our lord, Henry Fitz-Matilda. So they put constables and guards in the castle, and made great rejoicings. And they went thence to Brough and besieged it on all sides, and the first day they took the portcullis, and those within withdrew to the tower. Then they set fire to it, but when the defenders saw that, they surrendered to the King. But one knight was but that day newly come, and when his companions rendered themselves up, he went back to the tower and took two shields and held the battlements long; and he threw three javelins, and with each he killed a Scot. And when they failed him he threw all he could find upon them, confounding them all, and shouting, 'You are all conquered!' But when the fire burnt his shield he was forced to surrender. So Brough was taken; at which Robert de Vaux was somewhat dismayed. And he sent a messenger to Richard de Lucy; but de Lucy encouraged him, saying, that within fifteen days he would have news of the King.

Now the Bishop of Winchester, at the prayer of de Lucy, had gone over the sea and came to King Henry, and said to him, 'Richard de Lucy and the other barons who hold to you salute you by me; but hear the truth,—there are not ten who hold to you in right loyalty.'

Then said the King, 'What is Richard de Lucy doing then? Is he on my side?'

'Yes, sire, truly; he would rather let himself be bound with cords than fail you.'

'And the Earl of Arundel,—is he with me, or making war against me?'

'Sire, he is ever foremost in all your affairs.'

'And Humphrey de Bohun,—is he fighting my enemies?'

'Sire, he is one of the most loyal to you.'

'De Stuteville, does he still hold his castle?'

'Sire, De Stutevilles are never traitors.'

'And the Bishop elect of Lincoln, can he not fight against his enemies?'

'Sire, he is truly your friend, and has knights and good soldiers enough?'

'Thomas Fitz-Bernard and his brother,—do they go with Richard de Lucy?'

'In truth, sire, if it please you, they are your good friends, and Roger Bigod, who never failed you.'

'But tell me truly of my land in the north; has not Roger de Stuteville come to terms?'

'A thousand men would die, sire, an evil death before Roger would do you wrong!'

'Ralph de Glanville,—is he at Richmond, and Sir Robert de Vaux? What do those two barons?'

Then the messenger heaved a deep sigh, and the King asked again, 'Wherefore sigh you? Is Robert de Vaux a traitor? Has he given up Carlisle?'

'Nay, he holds it nobly, like a gentle baron; but it is right to tell you of his danger. The King of Scotland came riding by Carlisle the other day, and with great threats demanded that Sir Robert de Vaux should give up the castle to him, covenanting to give him great gifts; but if he refused, he would starve them all, little and great.'

'By my faith!' said the King, 'here is a good covenant. "In little time God works," as the beggar says. What did the Scot do? did he besiege Carlisle?'

'Nay, sire, if it please you, but he took Appleby and the Castle of Brough.'

'How!' said the King, 'is Appleby taken?'

'Yes, sire, in truth, and all the country round; and it has greatly rejoiced your mortal enemies. Sire, I am come from Robert de Vaux, for he can get neither wine nor corn; nor can he get aid from Richmond. If he is not succoured quickly, all will be famished, and Northumberland will be altogether wasted, and Odonel de Umfraville disinherited, and New Castle upon Tyne overwhelmed, and William de Vesci lose his lands; for the Scots, like evil spirits, overrun everything.'

Then said the King with tears and deep sighs, 'Nay, that would be an evil thing. But what does the Bishop of Durham?'

'He is agreed with King William.'

'Saint Thomas guard my kingdom!' said the King. 'But tell me, what of the barons of my city of London?'

'They are the most loyal people of your kingdom. There is none in the town of age to bear arms that is not very well armed. But Gilbert de Montfichet has fortified his castle, and says that the Clares are allied with him.'

'Then God guard my barons of London!' said the King. 'But go back, Sir Bishop, to your country. If God give me health, you shall have me in London within fifteen days, and I will take vengeance on all my enemies.' And he summoned his people to meet him at Rouen.

So the Bishop returned, and Richard de Lucy came to ask news of the King. 'Sir,' said the Bishop, 'he is a king of worth indeed, and fears neither Flemings nor the King of St. Denis; you will see him here in fifteen days.' Then Richard de Lucy was glad, and sent to bid Robert de Vaux not to fear, for he would have succour from the King; and Robert rejoiced greatly.

How King William was taken prisoner.

Then the same day came the King of Scotland before the town and demanded that Carlisle city and tower should be given up, or he would take it by force. To that answered Robert de Vaux, 'Set me a time,—name me a day; and if the King, my lord, does not succour me, I will render up the castle.' And said King William, 'You will have no succour; I have no fear of that.' And he went to the Odonel's castle, wishing to surprise him; but the castle was newly fortified and he had good men and strong; but his people, knowing the great hatred that the King of Scotland bore him, made him go out of his castle. So, with a heavy heart, he departed. And the host of Scotland, Flemings, and Borderers, came and assailed the castle with great noise and shouting, but those within defended themselves bravely.

But Odonel rode on his hairy bay to seek for succour, and he wandered about night and day on his good brown horse till he had got together four hundred valiant knights, with shining helmets, to succour Prudhoe with their sharp swords. And the siege lasted three days, as I know; and Odonel's good men within defended themselves so well, that their enemies gained not of the castle the worth of a silver penny; but the fields were destroyed and the gardens trampled by these evil men; and when they could do no more, it came into their minds to bark the apple-trees.

Then King William, perceiving there was no more to be done, said to his counsellors, 'Let us go to Alnwick and leave this. We will let our Scots waste the sea-coast, and woe be to them if they leave house or minster standing; and the men of Galloway shall go another way and kill the men in Odonel's lands; and we will go and besiege Alnwick, and the land shall be destroyed.' So on Friday morning the trumpets sounded and the host departed; and he came to Alnwick, and the Scots wasted and burnt all the land, and the church of St. Laurence was violated and three hundred men killed.

But Odonel rode with his proud companions, William de Stuteville and Ralph de Glanville, Sir Bernard de Baliol and William de Vesci. The Archbishop of York sent sixty knights of his retinue. And he came to New Castle upon Tyne at dead of night, and he heard news of the King of Albany that he was at Alnwick with few men, for the Scots were spread over the country, burning and wasting. Then the knights took counsel together, whether they should attack him ; and Odonel said, 'Shame be to him who refuses ! I will be first, for he has done me great harm. If he wait for us to attack him, he will be discomfited.' And Bernard de Baliol said, 'Who has not boldness enough deserves neither honour nor lands.' And Ralph de Glanville, 'Let us be wise and send a spy to see how many they be, and we will come after.'

So Odonel called his men, and they came by night to Alnwick ; and the knights of the King of Scotland said to him, 'Northumberland is yours, whoever may laugh or weep.' But he answered, 'Let us wait for our host, and then assault the castle.' And because of the heat he took off his helmet and sat down to eat, and his servants brought him food there before the castle. But our knights were hidden by a mist, and their spy came to them, and related to them what he had seen. 'Then seize your arms!' cried Ralph de Glanville, 'and fear nothing ;' and they mounted their horses in haste, and took their arms. The King was brave, daring, and bold, and he stood unarmed before Alnwick.

I tell the tale as one who was there, for I saw it myself. And one raised the war-cry of 'Vesci,' and 'Glanville knights,' and 'Baliol' others, and Odonel and de Stuteville raised their cries. But the King, undismayed, armed himself in haste, and mounted a fleet horse, and rode to the fight. And he brought the first to the ground, and made a fierce assault ; but one rushed upon him, and with a lance pierced through his horse, and the King and his horse fell to the ground, and the horse fell upon him, so that he could not rise, but lay unable to help himself and his men ; and the battle was strong and fierce on both sides. Great slaughter was made of the Flemings, and many will never cry 'Arras!' more. But the King lay beneath his horse, and thus I, with my own eyes, saw him taken, as he surrendered to Ralph de Glanville, and all his bravest knights were taken. But our knights, loving not the Flemings, slew them all. So the King gave himself up to Ralph, for what else could he do? And Ralph was glad, for he saw that the war was at an end, and England would have peace. And he took off his armour and mounted him up on a palfrey, and led him away to New Castle upon Tyne.

Now the battle was fought well on both sides. Sir Roger de Mowbray and Sir Adam de Port fled away in haste, for all were their enemies, and if they were taken there would be no safety for them. Sir Alan de Lanceles defended himself as long as he could. He was very old, and had not jousted for thirty years ; but he was taken, and will have to pay great ransom, for he was very rich. And William de Mortimer did well that day, going through the ranks like a wild boar. He met Sir Bernard de Baliol, and bore him down and his horse, and made him yield. And Raoul le Rus did well ; but more than a hundred assailed him, so no marvel he surrendered, but he will pay dearly for this war. And Richard Maluvel took and gave great blows, fearing none while he was on horseback, for he had a good horse, and he did as much as thirteen men; but he lost his horse, for it was wounded, and fell, and numbers came upon him crying, 'Surrender, quickly!' So he was forced to yield in bitterness of soul. But it would be too long to tell you of all who were taken, for there were near a hundred whom William de Vesci put to ransom, besides the prisoners of Bernard de Baliol, Walter de Bolebec, Odonel, and the others.

But it was no marvel they were discomfited, for there lay at St. Laurence the bodies of those whom the Scotch had murdered; and they had wounded and ill-treated more than a thousand, that there was weeping, and mourning, and tears. For that sin King William was that day discomfited. So he was lodged that night at New Castle, and the next day Ralph de Glanville took him and brought him to Richmond, where he should sojourn till King Henry made known his pleasure.

How the tidings were brought to King Henry.

Now the King was come by this time to England, and came to St. Thomas at Canterbury, and confessed himself a sinner and repentant, and took his penance. Then he departed and came to London; for he had great desire to see his city and his good people. But his heart was heavy for the Scotch war. But when they heard in London of his coming, each one attired himself in his richest garments, apparelling himself in rich cloth of silk, and every one had an ambling palfrey, and issued forth of the city. Sir Henry le Blunt was the first to kiss the King's hand; but you might have gone a league while the King was receiving his barons. And he thanked them much, saying, they were very loyal men.

'Sire,' said Gervaise Suplest, 'let be; may the day never come when any can call the Londoners traitors! They would rather have their limbs cut off than commit treason.'

'Certainly,' said the King, 'they have a right to boast; and I will requite them, if they have any need of me.'

So they conveyed the King to Westminster, and rejoiced at the coming of their lord, and gave him presents, and did him honour. Yet he was sad still, because of the King of Scotland and Sir Roger de Mowbray, who were destroying his lands. But before the right time for going to bed came, there came to him glad tidings. Now, he was entered into his chamber, and was suffering much—for he had not eaten nor drunk for three days of the week, nor slept with his eyes shut, but had travelled day and night. So he was leaning on his elbow, and slumbering a little, while a servant rubbed his feet. And all was silent: there was no noise, nor any one speaking, nor harp nor viol sounding, when a messenger came to the door and called softly.

Then the chamberlain said, 'Who is there?'

'I am a messenger, friend. Sir Ralph de Glanville has sent me to speak to the King of a great matter.'

And the chamberlain said, 'Leave the matter till to-morrow.'

'By my faith!' said the messenger, 'but I must speak to him at once. My lord is sad at heart; let me enter, good chamberlain!'

But the chamberlain said, 'I dare not do it. The King is asleep.'

But at those words the King awoke, and heard some one crying at the door, 'Open! open!'

'Who is that?' said the King.

'Sire,' answered the chamberlain, 'it is a messenger from the north. I know him well. He is Ralph de Glanville's man; Brien is his name.'

'By my faith!' said the King, 'he wants aid. Let him come in.'

So the messenger entered and saluted the King, saying, 'God save you, Sir King! You first, and then your friends.'

'Brien,' said the King, 'what news do you bring? Has the King of Scotland entered Richmond, taken New Castle upon Tyne? Odonel de Umfraville is taken or driven out, and all my barons chased out of their lands? Tell me the truth. They have served me badly, if I do not avenge them.'

'Sire,' said the messenger, 'listen to me a little. Your barons in the north are good men enough, and my lord sends you by me love and greeting, and my lady too; and he says by me that you need not bestir yourself, for the King of Scotland is taken and all his barons.'

Then said King Henry, 'Are you speaking truth?'

'Yea, sire, truly; by the morning you will know it. For the Archbishop of York will send you two private messengers; but I came first, knowing the truth. I have not slept for four days past, nor eaten nor drunk, and I am very famished. I pray you give me a reward.'

And the King replied, 'You need not doubt of that. If you have spoken truly, you shall be rich enough. But tell me the truth: Is the King of Scotland taken?'

'On my faith, sire, yea! Hang me by a rope, burn me at a stake, if I am not proved true before midday to-morrow!'

'Then God be praised!' said the King; 'and St. Thomas the Martyr, and all the saints!'

So the messenger went to his lodging, and had plenty to eat and drink. And the King was so glad at heart, that he went to his knights and woke them all, saying, 'Barons, awake! I have that to tell you will make you glad. The King of Scotland is taken; they tell me it is true tidings.'

And his knights answered, 'Now God be thanked, the war is finished, and your kingdom at peace!'

The next day, before noon, came one named Roger from the Archbishop of York; and the King was glad when he saw they both said the same. And he took a little stick and gave it to Brien, that he should have ten liveries of his land for the labour he had had.

Then he sent messengers to David, brother of the King of Scotland; and he was at Leicester, like a bold vassal. And the King sent him word that the game was played out, that there was nothing for him but to yield and come to his mercy. And David knew no better counsel than to give up the castle and come to the King. Eight days were enough for all this; and the King had peace, and his enemies were taken.

But the news came that Rouen is besieged; so he tarried no longer, but passed the sea, taking David with him. And Brien returned to his lord, and told his lord how the King would have him bring the King of Scotland with haste to Southampton. And the King Henry tarried at Southampton for a good wind, and Sir Ralph de Glanville made haste to come, leading with him the King of Scotland, sad at heart. But when they came thither, King Henry was in Normandy; but he had left command that he should cross in haste, and he tarried not.

Now the King came to Rouen at dawn of day; and by vespers peace was established, and the war was finished.

CHAPTER IV.

RICHARD CŒUR DE LION.

How Saladin took the Holy City, and how King Richard set out on a Crusade.

Now about the year 1187, it came to pass that the Christians in the land of Syria were, for their evil deeds, given over into the hand of Saladin, who had before made himself Sultan of Egypt and Damascus. He captured Acre, Berytus, and Sidon; and took prisoner Guy, king of Jerusalem, and advanced upon the Holy City itself. It soon fell into his hands, and all who could not ransom themselves were made slaves. But when the tidings of these calamities were brought by the Archbishop of Tyre into Europe, many were moved with compassion, and determined upon vengeance. And first of all Richard, earl of Poitou, assumed the cross; and after him his father, Henry II., king of England, and Philip, king of France, and great numbers of nobles and knights.

But before King Henry could set out on his journey to the Holy Land, he fell sick and died; and Earl Richard returned to England to be crowned king. He was a man tall of stature, with auburn hair, a commanding carriage, and limbs strong and well made for fighting, and long arms that were unequalled in wielding the sword. And he made haste to set his kingdom in order, and to collect material for the war, and passed over into France. He bade his ships sail round Spain and tarry for him at Messina, and with his chosen troops he marched to Vezelai, where he had appointed to meet King Philip.

When the two armies came together, they were so numerous that the hills were covered with the tents and pavilions, and it seemed as if a new city had arisen, bright with gay pennons and standards. There the two kings made a treaty, and swore to keep the peace towards one another; and the two armies set forward, and marched by Lyons to the sea in good fellowship and brotherly kindness.

King Philip had hired Genoese ships to carry him and his men to Messina; and he sailed in them, having engaged to tarry at Messina for the coming of King Richard. The English army rested at Marseilles three weeks, and then took ship and sailed between the islands of Sardinia and Corsica, and passed the burning mountains called Vulcano and Strango, and came to the city of Messina, where the ships of King Richard waited for them.

Now the king of the country, whose name was William, had lately died; and he had married King Richard's sister, but they had no children, and the kingdom had passed to Tancred. But the people of the country, who were commonly called Griffons, being many of them of Saracen blood, made themselves hostile to the men in our ships while they waited for King Richard, calling them dogs, and other evil names, and insulting them often, and even killing some of them as they had opportunity.

When King Richard's coming was known, all the people ran out to see him, for his fame was spread abroad; and the sea was covered with his galleys, glittering with arms and standards, and the prows of the galleys were painted each with its own sign, while the King himself was seen standing on a part of a ship higher and more gaily painted than the rest. And thus, with the pealing of trumpets and clarions, he came to land, and rode amid his own men and a crowd of the wondering people to his hostel.

Of the taking of the City of Messina, and the coming of the Princess Berengaria.

But the disputes between the pilgrims and the natives of the city grew hotter day by day, and when blood was shed in these quarrels, the two kings consulted with the governor of the city how peace should be maintained between them. But while they were in conference, there came messengers in great haste to the King Richard, saying that the people had attacked and were slaying his men. Then the King, mounting his horse in haste, rode out to stop the quarrel; but when he reached the place, the Lombards, mad with rage, railed upon him with loud cries. Then he drew his sword and attacked them,

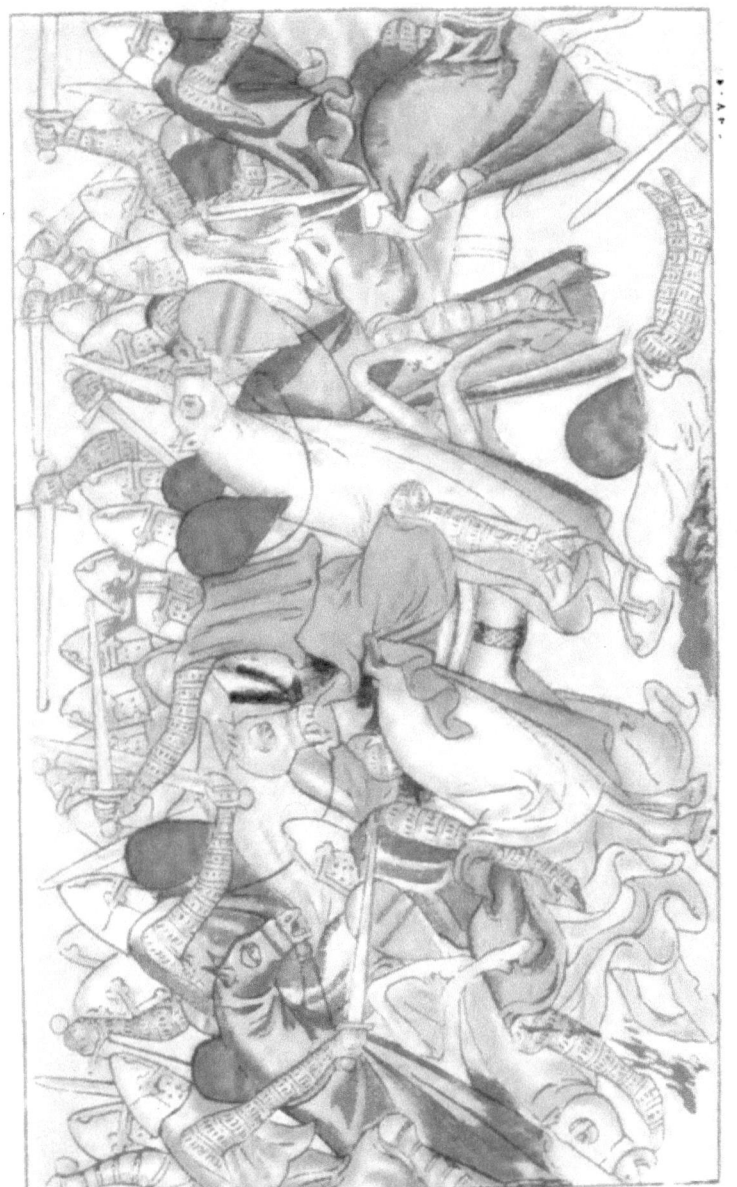

RICHARD CŒUR DE LION IN BATTLE.

and though he had but twenty men with him, they fled before him like sheep before the wolf and ran into their city and shut the gates. Some of them went to King Philip, and prayed him to come to their aid; and there are those who say he avowed himself more ready to help them than to fight for the King of England's men, to whom he was bound by oath.

Then King Richard, when he saw the gates shut against him, made a fierce assault upon the city, and they defended themselves with stones and darts from the walls, so that many of our men were slain. But the King, observing a postern neglected by the citizens, ordered an attack to be made upon it; and the gate was broken down, and thus the whole army entered the city. Great spoil fell into the hands of the victors, and many of the citizens were slain, but King Richard stopped the slaughter. Then when King Philip saw the standard of the King Richard on the walls of the city, he was moved with envy, and hated Richard in his heart. And he sent to him and bade him take down his standard and raise in its place the standard of France. To this Richard, angered, returned no answer; but his counsellors, fearing a breach between the kings, besought him to yield, and the standards of both the kings were raised on the walls.

King Philip sought also to inflame the mind of Tancred against Richard; but he, fearing the ill-will of so great a man, made peace and an alliance with him, and they met at the city of Fatina, midway between Palermo and Messina, and swore to keep faith with one another.

Then, it being now Christmastide, King Richard gave a great feast, and sent out a crier to invite all who would come. And with all respect he sent to the King of France; and he came with a great number of the nobles. The feast was held in the castle of Mategriffon, which the King had constructed to hold the city in awe, and was celebrated with great splendour. The dishes and platters were all of gold and silver, curiously wrought with the chisel and ornamented with precious stones. And when the feast was over, he sent the most beautiful cups to the King of France, and bade him choose which he would have; and to the nobles also he gave gifts according to their rank.

When the winter was past, King Philip made ready his ships, and set sail for the Holy Land; but King Richard stayed yet in Sicily. For tidings were brought him that his mother, Queen Eleanor, was coming to him, and with her was the noble daughter of the King of Navarre, whose name was Berengaria. For when Richard was yet Earl of Poitou, he had seen her and loved her, and the King, her father, sent her to him now, that he might marry her before he crossed the sea. So King Richard went out to meet them, and brought them with great joy to Messina.

Then King Richard made ready his ships to follow the King of France, and gave the care of them to Robert de Torneham. And the Princess Berengaria, with his sister, the widowed Queen of Sicily, he put on board a ship called a dromon. These are heavy ships and slow in sailing, but stronger and firmer than the galleys.

Then the great fleet put to sea with a fair breeze, and some rowing, and some sailing, passed out of the port of Messina; the dromons in the rear, and the galleys going slowly that they might keep with them. But our voyage was beset with perils and difficulties; for first the wind dropped so that we could not proceed, and then it rose against us and raged so furiously that the ships would not obey the pilots, but were driven hither and thither through the boiling sea. But while all the others were overcome with fear and distressed with grievous sickness, the King unmoved bade them not despair, and as he had the best sailors on board his ship, he caused them to light a great wax taper, and hoist it in a lantern on the mast, that the other ships might see it and follow him, as a hen gathers her chickens. And when the storm was over we came to Crete, and waited to collect the ships; but there were five-and-twenty that came not, at which the King was greatly moved.

Then, when the wind was favourable, we sailed away; but it rose again, and drove us upon the island of Rhodes, where we tarried certain days, and then went on our way. The royal ship being always first, the King perceived a very large ship called a buss bearing down, returning from Jerusalem, and those in the ship brought him tidings that the King of France was landed at Acre, and with all diligence was directing the siege.

Then King Richard hasted on his journey, but the wind being contrary, he could not make way, and the ship in which the two queens were was the first to reach Cyprus; but they dropped anchor outside the port, and feared to land. For there reigned now in that land a wicked tyrant who had usurped the name of emperor, of whom it was reported that he was in league and alliance with Saladin, and that in sign thereof they had drunk each other's blood. Then the storm still continuing to rage, three of the King's ships were broken to pieces on the shore, and many of those on board were drowned, among whom was the King's signet-bearer. His body being washed on shore, the signet was found and brought afterwards to the army for sale. Those who escaped and swam to shore, as well as all who ventured to land, were seized by the Griffons and stripped of their arms; neither would they allow them to return to their ships. But when the pilgrims saw that their lives were in danger they contrived to meet together in a body to fight their way back to the ships. They had no arms except three bows; but one of them named Roger de Hardecurt found a horse, and rode down all who opposed him, and William du Bois shot arrows upon them unceasingly, and so they advanced towards the shore. And the soldiers on board, seeing their danger, came in haste to their aid, and brought them in safety to the ships.

Of the coming of Richard to Cyprus.

The same day the Emperor came into the city of Limasol, and sought by craft and guile to allure the queens to land, sending them presents of bread and meat and the famed wine of Cyprus. They, fearing to offend him, gave their promise to come to land the next day, and, very solicitous for the safety of the fleet, of which they knew nothing, sat gazing out to sea, taking sad counsel with one another, when, behold! in the distance appeared two black things like crows; and as they came nearer they perceived that they were ships, and behind came another and another, until, to their great joy, King Richard, with all his fleet, appeared in sight.

Then, when King Richard had anchored in the port, it was told him how some of his ships had been broken, and how his men had been stripped and plundered by the Griffons. Being much angered, therefore, he sent two knights to the Emperor to demand restitution and satisfaction. But he scorned to yield any satisfaction to a king, and answered only with contempt and insult. So the King cried aloud, 'To arms!' and, with his men, sprang into the boats and rowed to seize the port. Then the Griffons blocked up the entrance with old galleys, and casks, and piles of old wood, to obstruct their landing; and the Emperor and his army took up their position on the shore. They made a brave show, with costly arms and rich, bright garments, and fine horses and mules, eager for battle. As our men approached they were assailed by slingers and archers from five galleys by the shore. But our men, unmoved, attacked the galleys and took them, and from them poured a shower of arrows on those who held the landing-place. The Griffons gave way a little space, but gaining higher ground, returned the arrows upon our men; and King Richard, seeing that his men durst not leave their boats, sprang himself into the water and ran boldly at the Griffons. His men, encouraged, followed him without delay, and fell with such force on the enemy that they gave way and fled. Then the King, finding a horse, mounted it and rode after the Emperor, crying to him to turn and meet him in single combat; but he turned not, and fled away.

Thus the King took the city of Limasol, and brought the queens to land, and rested until his horses could be brought from the ships. But the Emperor halted within two leagues, and when morning came he returned, and, with his army, took up his stand on a hill overlooking us. And a certain clerk, dismayed at the sight of so great a host, said to King Richard, 'My lord the King, in good truth it would be wisest to avoid meeting so great a multitude.' 'My lord clerk,' answered the King, 'keep to your Scriptures, and leave arms to us, and keep out of the crowd.' Then, with no more than fifty men, perceiving that the enemy hesitated, he rode upon them, and broke their line and dispersed them, and they fled in great dismay. He fell also upon the Emperor, and struck him from his horse, but he mounted another, and made haste to escape. And the enemy

RICHARD CŒUR-DE LION & THE EMPEROR OF CYPRUS

fled, and were overwhelmed by their pursuers, and the field was heaped with the slain. And the Emperor's banner was taken, and his tent, with all his silver and gold, and splendid raiment, and a great booty of horses and cattle and choice wine.

Then the King made a proclamation that all who would have peace might come to him in safety, and many forsook the Emperor, so that he fled for safety to a fort called Nicosia.

Of the Marriage of Richard and Berengaria and the Conquest of Cyprus.

Now about this time there came into the port three galleys, bringing King Guy of Jerusalem and his followers; and he had come to ask the help of King Richard against King Philip of France, who wished to depose him and make the Marquis Conrad king in his place. And King Richard received him kindly, and gave him great gifts.

Being now established in safety at Limasol, King Richard celebrated with great splendour his marriage with Berengaria, daughter of the King of Navarre, and there were present at the ceremony the Archbishop and the Bishop of Evreux, and a great concourse of nobles.

Then the Masters of the Hospitalers of Jerusalem brought about a meeting between the victorious king and the Emperor of Cyprus. The Emperor desired much to have peace, because for his cruelty his people hated him, and he feared to trust them. They met together in a plain near Limasol, and the King rode to the place on a Spanish horse of such beauty that no painter could have designed one more perfect in form. The King was clothed in a garment of rose colour, ornamented with rows of crescents of solid silver, and on his head a scarlet hat with beasts and birds worked in gold upon it. His saddle was of bright colour, spangled with gold, and behind were two golden lions with their mouths open about to attack one another. He wore golden spurs and a sword of proved metal with a golden hilt, and he rode like a noble soldier, so that all who saw him wondered at him.

Thus the King and the Emperor met and made peace, and the Emperor agreed to give up his castles into the hands of the King, and to send with him five hundred knights to fight for Jerusalem; and the King engaged to give back the castles if the Emperor kept faith. Moreover, the Emperor agreed to pay five hundred marks to those whom he had plundered. So they kissed one another and swore peace and friendship, and the King returned to Limasol, and sent to the Emperor the pavilion that he captured in the battle. But a knight named Pain de Caiffa went to the Emperor and falsely told him that King Richard purposed to seize him and throw him in chains. Therefore, moved with fear, he fled by night to his city of Famagusta. Thus the war broke out again, for the King pursued him in his galleys, and his army marched against him, being led by King Guy. The Emperor hid in the woods, and when the

King, having landed at Famagusta, marched upon Nicosia, he laid an ambush for him, and attacked him suddenly with seven hundred Greeks, shooting poisoned arrows at the King. Then King Richard, urging his horse, bore down upon him with his spear; but the Emperor fled away, and, being mounted on a horse unmatched for speed, escaped. The people of Nicosia opened their gates to the King, and he received them into his favour; but all who fell into the Emperor's hands were tortured and cruelly mutilated.

King Guy took two of the Emperor's castles, and the Emperor's daughter and all his treasure fell into his hands. So when the Emperor knew that his people hated him, and that his forts were taken, and his daughter, whom he loved tenderly, was a captive, he came and fell down at King Richard's feet and submitted himself to him; only he prayed him that he would not put him in iron chains. And the King, moved with pity, raised him up, and made him sit beside him, and gave him silver chains instead of iron ones, and brought his daughter to him.

Thus King Richard conquered Cyprus in fifteen days, and obtained great spoil of gold, and silver, and precious cloths. And to King Guy he committed the custody of the Emperor, and his little daughter he gave to the Queen that she might bring her up. And having appointed trusty men to transmit to him corn and meat, he took ship and sailed with all his fleet and the two queens for the Holy Land.

And as they came near the land, and were now

off Sidon, there appeared in sight a great ship filled with Saracens going to aid their countrymen in Acre. Then the King sent Peter des Barres, captain of one of his galleys, to ask who they were, and they answered that they belonged to the King of France. So the King came near to the ship, and it was of great size and strongly made, with three tall masts, and painted with red and yellow lines; but he saw no Christian standard, and he doubted in himself who they were. So he sent others again to ask whence they came, and they answered they were Genoese bound for Tyre. Then the sailors were assured that they were Saracens, and at the King's command a galley rowed after them quickly; and when the Saracens saw that they did not salute them, they began to throw darts at them. So the King bade attack the ship; but as our men rowed round it, it seemed so high, and strong, and well defended, that they feared to begin. But the King, chiding their cowardice, urged them to the attack, and some of them sprang into the water and bound the rudder with cords to stop the ship, and, climbing up the cables, leapt on board. The Turks met them bravely, cutting off their hands as they clung to the ship and flinging them back into the sea.

The fight lasted long; the Turks were driven back to the prow, but new defenders came from within the ship, and the Christians were forced back into their galleys. Then the King bade them row the galleys against the ship's side and strike it with their iron beaks, and thus they pierced the ship's sides and it began to fill. Thirty-five of the Turks, who were men of consequence or of skill in handling machines, the King saved alive, but the rest were killed, or perished in the water.

Of the coming of Richard to Acre, and the taking of the City.

Then the King, after this victory, sailed on till he came in sight of Acre. And there, round the walls, lay the great army of the besiegers, from every Christian land under heaven; and beyond it might be seen, dispersed upon the hills and in the valleys and plains, the brightly coloured tents of the Turkish army. There was the pavilion of Saladin himself, and of his brother Saphadin, and of Kahadin, the mainstay of Paganism. It was the Saturday in the Pentecost week that King Richard landed at Acre, and the earth shook with the exultant shouts of the Christians. The day was kept as a festival, and far into the night was heard the sound of the trumpets and pipes and the songs of the rejoicing soldiers while the darkness was dispersed by the glare of torches till the Turks thought the valley was on fire. But the Turks were much cast down and dejected.

But after a few days the King fell sick, and his sickness was so sore that he could not go out to fight, though he busied himself with preparation of machines of war. The King of France then, not willing to wait till King Richard should be recovered, on the Monday after the Feast of Saint John the Baptist bade make a great assault on the city. Then the Turks within made a great clamour and beat platters and timbrels to call upon Saladin to come to their aid. And his men fell upon us and fought so fiercely that the pilgrims were forced to give up the attack on the city to defend themselves; and those in the city threw Greek fire on the machines of the King of France and destroyed them. Then the King Philip fell sick from vexation and confusion.

And when he was recovered, he made new machines, and one there was which he called 'Bad neighbour.' And the Turks had one which they called 'Bad kinsman,' and which often broke Bad neighbour; but the King built it again, and with it he broke down part of the wall and shook the tower Maledictum. And the other leaders had also machines which did much harm to the Turks; and there was one petraria called the 'Petraria of God,' for a priest stood by it preaching and gathering money to work it. King Richard had two which were worked unceasingly; and he constructed others to shoot at great distances,—one called 'Berefred,' covered with hides, and so strong that it could not be broken or burnt. From one of his engines he shot into the city a great stone which he had brought from Messina, which killed twelve men with its blow. And besides the engines for throwing stones, the King of France had made one for scaling the walls, which was called the 'Cat,' because it crept up the walls and held on to it; and a cercleia, which was a shelter of hides under which he could sit and shoot at the city; but the Turks burnt the cat and the cerclcia with Greek fire. King Richard caused himself to be carried in a silken bed and laid under a cerclcia that thence he might shoot from his arbalest and encourage his men, and he promised them rewards for every stone they should displace from the wall. And many men fell by his arbalest, and among them a Turk who was dressed in the armour of a Christian whom he had slain.

Then the Turks, finding that their walls were shaken by undermining and by the blows of the machines, and many of their men slain in the assaults, sent two of their leaders to treat, offering to give up the city if they might leave it with all their arms and goods. King Philip gave his assent, but King Richard would not agree, after so long a siege, to win back a deserted city. Then many of the Turks in their fear escaped from the beleaguered city, and coming to the Christians, besought baptism that they might thus escape from destruction.

But Saladin, perceiving that it would be vain to hope that the city could hold out longer, consented that they should make peace on what terms they could. Then the chief men in the city went to the Christian kings and offered to give up the city, and the Holy Cross, and two hundred and fifty captives if they might depart from the city in their shirts only, leaving behind them all their arms and goods and paying for their ransom 200,000 Saracen talents; and to these terms the kings gave consent. So, having given up their noblest men as hostages, and having bound themselves by an oath to deliver the Holy

Cross and the captives within a month's space, they departed out of the city; and our men marvelled much to witness their composed countenances, unsubdued by adversity and the loss of all their goods.

And when the Turks were all departed out of the city, the Christians marched into it with shouts of joy and triumph and songs of praise, and the kings set up their banners on the walls and divided the city between them,—King Philip had the palace of the Templars, and King Richard the royal palace, into which the queens entered with their handmaids.

Of the departure of the King of France and the march of the army.

Then arose great discord between the kings touching King Guy and the Marquis, for King Philip wished to give all to the Marquis. And the quarrel grew hot between them; but by the princes' mediation, it was agreed that the Marquis should have the government of Tyre and should become king when King Guy should die; and it was further agreed that if the Marquis should die while King Richard were in that land, the crown should be left to him to dispose of as he should see best. Thus peace was made between them. But King Philip determined to return to his own land, saying he was sick; and though his men murmured sore and pleaded with him to remain, he embarked in a galley that he had begged of King Richard, and sailed away on St. Peter's Day, having sworn to do no harm nor damage to the men or lands of the King of England while he was absent in the Holy Land.

King Richard tarried at Acre repairing the walls, and waiting until Saladin should fulfil his covenant and send back the Cross and the captives, but when the time was now passed, and he saw that the unbelievers would not keep to their promises, he commanded that the hostages should be put to death, and that the army should make ready to go to Ascalon. But the Marquis withdrew himself to Tyre, and would no longer stay with the army. And as our army began to move out of the camp they were attacked by the Turks, and the Count of Hungary and King Richard's Marshal, Hugh of Poitou, were carried away prisoners, though the King fought hard to save them. But the Turks, not being oppressed with heavy armour, rode more swiftly than the Christians could, and, like flies, fled away when the King attacked them, but returned as soon as he stopped.

On the feast of St. Bartholomew the army, having passed out of the city, was drawn up on the seashore. The King led the vanguard and the Normans guarded the Standard. It was like the mast of a ship, bound with iron and fixed on four wheels, with the banner of the King floating on the top. The French, led by the Duke of Burgundy, were in the rear. Thus the army marched along the sea-shore, the Turks watching from the heights. And as the Christians came to a narrow way and were in confusion, the Saracens attacked them suddenly and a fierce fight began. One of the Bishop of Salisbury's men, by name Everard, had his right hand cut off by a Turk, but, without changing countenance, he seized his sword with his left hand and closed with the enemies that were pressing on him. Then King Richard riding to the spot drove off the Turks and made them flee to the mountains.

Now on this march the Christians were sore troubled by a venomous animal called Tarrentes, which by night stung them much, and the place which was stung swelled greatly and was filled with pain. But observing the matter, it was perceived that the Tarrentes feared greatly loud noises, and by beating together their basons and platters and other instruments the pilgrims drove them away.

Thus they marched till they came to Cæsarea, constantly fearing the attacks of the Turks, and suffering much from heat and weariness, so that many fell dead by the way. And each night ere they lay down to rest, one cried aloud in the midst of the camp, 'Help for the Holy Sepulchre!' and they all, with many tears, holding up their hands to heaven, cried, 'Help for the Holy Sepulchre!'

Then the pilgrims, leaving Cæsarea, came to the Dead River and passed on to the Salt River, and the Turks kept near and shot darts and arrows upon them as thick as hail. King Richard was wounded in the side by a dart, and the horses died fast. From the Salt River they came to the forest of Arsur, and by the river there waited for them the army of the Turks innumerable.

Of the Battle of Arsur and the wonderful victory of the Christians.

King Richard marshalled his army, the Templars being in the first rank, the men of Brittany and Anjou next after them, then the men of Poitou, under King Guy, and the Normans and the English with the Standard, and, last of all, a chosen body of Hospitallers. And so closely were they ordered that an apple could not have fallen among them without touching man or horse. King Richard and the Duke of Burgundy, with some chosen men, rode up and down to watch the Turks.

About nine o'clock in the morning a great multitude of Turks, in number about 10,000, came upon the Christians in a furious assault, throwing darts and arrows and shouting horribly. Among them were men very black in colour, and also the Saracens who live in the desert, called Bedouins, very rapid in their movements and carrying bows and arrows and a round shield. Behind them came the squadrons of the Turks with ensigns on their lances. There seemed to be more than 20,000 of them, and they came like lightning, raising a cloud of dust, so that they darkened all the heavens; and they had trumpets and horns, cymbals and gongs, making a horrible, discordant clamour. They came upon us from the side of the sea and from the side of the land, and they seemed to cover all the ground for a distance of two miles.

The pilgrims, hemmed in on all sides, marched on in a compact body, while the Turks assailed them before and behind, repelling their attacks as well as they were able without leaving the body. They suffered greatly from the heat and from the pressure, for they were scarce able to breathe; and the Hospitallers, being in the rear, could not return the blows, but marched on, bearing the blows of the Turks, which fell on their armour as on an anvil. But the Christians' courage did not fail, and the Turks cried aloud that 'they were made of iron.'

At last the Hospitallers were unable to endure patiently any longer, and the Marshal and another knight, named Baldwin de Carreo, broke from the ranks and rode at the enemy, crying to St. George for aid. They were followed by all the Hospitallers, so that the rear was soon in the front of the army. Then the Count of Champagne and Jacques d'Avennes Count Robert of Dreux and the Bishop of Beauvais, his brother, and many others, charged fiercely upon the Saracens. The Turks gave way before them, and the ground was strewn with the slain. The King, bursting through the Hospitallers, cut out a path for himself among the enemy, mowing them down as a reaper does the corn.

Thus the Turks were overcome and dispersed, and their army turned into a crowd of fugitives, but when our men ceased from the pursuit they gathered together again, and more than 20,000, armed with heavy maces, began the battle again. They were led by a kinsman of Saladin, named Takieddin, a bitter hater of the Christians, and he had with him more than 700 chosen men of valour of the body-guard of Saladin, bearing yellow banners. They fell upon a body of the Christians before they had fallen into their ranks round the Standard, and overwhelming them with their numbers grievously distressed them. But a brave knight, named William des Barres, with his men, attacked the Turks, and King Richard seeing their dangerous position mounted a bay Cyprian horse and rode into their midst and drove all before him.

The enemy fled away, and the Christians, gathering round the Standard, marched forward till they came to Arsur. There they pitched their tents, but ere the camp was formed a large body of Turks fell upon the rearguard. But King Richard, hearing the cry of his men, ran hastily to the place with only fifteen of his followers, crying with a mighty voice, 'O God, help us and the Holy Sepulchre!' At which his men hasted to follow him, and drove away the Turks, pursuing them to the walls of Arsur and cutting down many as they fled. And of those who fell on that day there were found on the field of battle the bodies of thirty-two Turks, whom, from the splendour of their armour, the Christians thought to be mighty chiefs, besides many lesser captains. Of the Christians fell but few, but there died there the great captain Jacques d'Avennes, who, having fallen from his horse, was surrounded by the Turks and overcome. And the Christians, mourning greatly for his fall, sent a company of Hospitallers and

Templars the next day to seek for his body, and they found it covered with wounds, and around lay the bodies of fifteen Turks whom he had slain ere he died. Then they bore him back to Arsur, and buried him there with great weeping, and wailing, and lamentation.

The great battle of Arsur spread dismay in the hearts of the Turks, and the name of Melech Ric was feared throughout the land. Then Saladin gave command to pull down the walls of the fortresses, lest King Richard should take them and make himself strong in them. And when the Christians were come to the city of Joppa, lo! the city was destroyed, that they could find no lodging there, and they encamped in an olive-garden without the town, and refreshed themselves with the figs and grapes and pomegranates and citrons that grew in the land.

How William de Pratelles gave himself up for the King, and of the deeds of the Earl of Leicester.

Then tidings came that the Turks were pulling down the walls of Ascalon, and King Richard counselled to march at once thither and save it. But the French wished rather to rebuild Joppa, and their counsel prevailed. But while they tarried there the Christians gave themselves to sloth and ease.

About this time it happened that King Richard, having ridden to take his pastime in hawking, and having with him but few of his men, being wearied with his sport, lay down and fell asleep. And while he slept there came suddenly upon him a company, hoping to make him prisoner. The King awakened by the noise threw himself on his horse, and his attendants following him, drove off the assailants, but they in fleeing drew him to a spot where lay other Turks hidden. The King being surrounded by them fought bravely and defended himself well, but there were so many of them that he would have fallen into their hands, had not one of his knights, named William de Pratelles, cried out that he was the Melech, and the Turks hearing his words seized him and carried him away prisoner. Thus the King had time to escape, and when he came to the town he found his soldiers coming out to his help, for they had heard of his danger. Then he returned and pursued the Turks, hoping to set free William de Pratelles, but they were got away. Then the soldiers prayed the King not to endanger his life any more. Nevertheless he was ever the first to attack and the last to retreat.

Then the King, with a part of the army, went to rebuild the forts of Plans and Maen, which the Turks had destroyed. And it fell out one day that they had gone out to gather fodder for their horses, and while the esquires were busy gathering it, the Templars kept guard over them. Then there fell suddenly upon them a company of 4000 horsemen, which when they saw they dismounted, and standing back to back, defended themselves as well as they could. And when three of them were fallen, there came to their aid Andrew de Chamgui and fifteen knights; but the Turks continued to attack them. Then the

King, hearing the noise, sent to their help the Count de Saint Paul and the Earl of Leicester, and seizing his arms followed them. Then the Earl of Leicester came and saved two whom they had taken prisoners, and distinguished himself by his bravery. But when the King reached the place, the battle was still raging, for the enemy was so many in number; and some of his men, seeing the strength of the enemy, counselled him to save himself, and not attempt to rescue his men. But the King, growing red with anger, answered, 'What! Shall I send my men on to fight, promising to come and help them, and then leave them in the battle? I should not be worthy of the name of a king.' And without another word he spurred his horse and fell with such force into the thickest ranks of the Turks, that he broke their array and rode through them, cutting down on all sides, and returning dispersed them all; and, among many others, a great admiral, named Aralchais, fell by his hand. And the whole company fled, and the Christians returned with some prisoners to the camp.

When the castles were now about to be finished, King Richard sent ambassadors to Saladin to demand that the land of Syria should be given up, and that the kingdom of Babylon should pay tribute. Saladin, being crafty, would not refuse the King's demand, but deluded him with promises, and sent his brother Saphadin to him with rich gifts. And there arose a murmuring among the Christians that King Richard was friendly to the Gentiles. But when the King saw that the promises of Saphadin were vain, he would no longer listen to him, but fought more bravely than before to wipe out the reproaches that were brought against him.

The Earl of Leicester, attacking a large company of Turks with but few men, made them flee before him; but three of his knights, pursuing them with too great boldness, were taken prisoners, which when the Earl perceived, he rode to their aid. He had driven them over a river, when 500 fresh Turks came up and surrounded him. Many of his knights were wounded, and he himself was thrown off his horse and nearly drowned in the river. But two of his knights succoured him; and one of them, named Robert of Newbury, gave him his own horse. Though they fought as long as they could, the numbers were so great that they could defend themselves no longer; but holding by the necks of their horses, and bearing silently the rain of blows, were led away prisoners. But aid was near. Andrew de Chamgui and other knights came spurring to the spot, and the fortune of battle turned against the Turks. The Earl fought fiercely. Two horses were killed under him. Never did so small a man perform such great deeds; and at last victory stayed with him.

Of the rebuilding of Ascalon, and the discord among the Christians.

The castle being now repaired, the army of the Christians was commanded to leave the plains and to march to the foot of the mountains, that they might be ready to go up to Jerusalem. And Saladin, being aware of it, went himself to Jerusalem, giving command to his army to occupy the mountains; and there fell upon the Christians a storm of rain and hail, which blew down the tents and did great damage to the food, spoiling the biscuits and bacon. Many of the horses also were drowned in the flood, and the armour and coats-of-mail became so rusty that it needed much labour to make them bright again. Many, also, of the pilgrims fell sick. But so great was their joy at the hope of seeing Jerusalem, that they bore their sufferings with cheerfulness, and eagerly desired to continue the march. Neither would the sick be left behind, but caused themselves to be borne in litters; and some of them fell into the enemies' hands, and were martyred without mercy.

But the Templars and Hospitallers, and the wise men, prayed King Richard not to march yet to Jerusalem, for they feared that the siege would be long, and the army in the mountains would do them hurt. Neither if the city were captured had they men with whom to garrison it, for all longed sore to return home. They counselled rather to defer the siege of Jerusalem until the walls of Ascalon should be rebuilt. And when it was known that their counsel had prevailed, the pilgrims grieved sore, and cried out curses on those evil counsellors; and it seemed now impossible to bear the sufferings from the rain and want of food, which a little before had seemed so light. Many of them left the army, especially of the French, going to Acre or Joppa, or joining the Marquis at Tyre.

But King Richard, with his nephew the Count Henry of Champagne, and the rest of the army, marched in great suffering and distress to Ascalon; and Saladin, hearing that the Christians had returned to the sea-shore, sent his army to their homes. And the King, by entreaties and persuasion, drew back to the camp those who had forsaken it; and they began to rebuild the city of Ascalon. All worked together, side by side; princes and nobles carried the stones, and clerks and laymen, knights and retainers, built together. The King himself was active in the work, building with his own hands, and encouraging his men, and giving money to those who were in need.

At that time the King, going one day to reconnoitre the fort of Darum, came suddenly upon a body of Turks who were taking Christian captives for sale. And when they saw the King's banner they fled in dismay, and got them safe into the fort, leaving the captives without; and the King came and set them free. There were twelve thousand men who were thus saved by the King from slavery.

But the discord waxed strong in the Christian camp; and the Duke of Burgundy went away and came to Acre. And he found the city in disorder, for the party of King Guy was fighting with the party of the Marquis. Then the Marquis sailed in his galley to Acre, hoping to take possession of the city, but his adversaries sent and prayed to King Richard to come to their aid. The Marquis in haste returned to Tyre, and King Richard quieted and appeased the people. And when he could not prevail upon the Marquis to be at peace with him, and help in the war with Saladin, he took counsel with the leaders in the army, and adjudged him to have lost all right to his kingdom. But the French joined with the Marquis, and seven hundred soldiers left the camp at Ascalon and marched away from the camp.

While the King tarried at Acre, there came to him the son of Saphadin, that the King might make him a knight; and on Palm Sunday, with great magnificence, the King girded him with the belt of knighthood.

Then the King, having celebrated the feast of Easter at Ascalon with great feasting and rejoicing, and the city being rebuilt, went out to reconnoitre Gaza. But Saladin assembled his army and prepared for war; and he was greatly encouraged because of the departure of the French, and trusted soon to recover Acre and Tyre.

How the Marquis Conrad was chosen King, and how he was slain by two young men.

But before the war was begun again there landed in the country the Prior of Hereford, and he came with evil tidings to King Richard. For Earl John, the King's brother, had driven out of England the King's Chancellor, and the others whom the King had appointed to govern in his absence, and had seized the King's revenues, and made the nobles swear allegiance to him. Then the King assembling the leaders of the army told them of the tidings, and that he must return to his own land, but would leave three hundred knights and two thousand footsoldiers, to fight at his cost. And they prayed him, before he left the country, to appoint a new king, that they might be no longer divided, but should follow one leader; and they entreated on their bended knee that the Marquis might be made king, for that he could better defend the kingdom than another. And the King listened to their request, though the Marquis was his enemy, and indeed a traitor, for at that time he was secretly plotting to make peace with Saladin, as it was fully known afterwards.

And the chief men in the army went to Tyre to bring the Marquis with honour, and he was filled with joy at his election, and made great preparation to celebrate his coronation worthily. But it fell out that as he was returning from a feast, merry and cheerful, there ran upon him suddenly two young men, assassins, with knives in their hands, and stabbed him to the heart. And one of them, before he was put to death, being questioned, confessed that he had been sent by the Old Man of Musse to assassinate the Marquis, whom he judged worthy of death. For the Old Man brought up in his palace many noble boys, and taught them many things, that when they were grown up he might send them whither he would, that they might do his will. And when he would that a great man should die he gave them a poniard, sharp and long, and bade them go murder him for remission of their sins.

Thus the Marquis died, before he was crowned king, amid great lamentation, having given command to his wife not to give up the city of Tyre to anyone but King Richard. But there came to Tyre at that time Count Henry of Champagne, nephew of King Richard, who was one of those whom he had sent to fetch the Marquis, and when the people saw him they cried out that he should be their king; and when they entreated him, he replied that he would do nothing without the consent of King Richard. Then messengers were sent to apprise the King of these things: how the Marquis was slain, and how the people had chosen Count Henry king. And when the King heard of the death of the Marquis, he was silent a long time, being astonished at his sudden and violent end, but the election of Count Henry pleased him much. So Count Henry was made king, and married the widow of the Marquis, who was the heiress of the kingdom, and having taken possession of his forts and castles, made haste to come to the aid of King Richard in the war. But when King Richard remembered King Guy, he had compassion on him, and he made him ruler of Cyprus.

Now while the King Richard still tarried, waiting for the King Henry, he rode out every day to attack the Turks, and he killed many with his own hand and took many captive. And it happened one day, as he was riding along the road, there came out a wild boar and stood in his way. He was of immense size, and terrible to behold, and he was foaming at the mouth with rage. His bristles stood up, and he seemed about to attack. Then the King attacked him with his spear, and drove it into his side, but it broke with his weight, and, mad with rage, he rushed at the King. The King had not time to get out of his way, so he spurred his horse and leaped clear over him; only the trappings of the horse were torn by the boar's tusks, and as he leapt he struck the boar on the head and stunned it, and then, wheeling round quickly, put it to death.

How King Richard captured Darum and prepared to go up to Jerusalem.

Then there came again messengers to the King from England, and some prayed him much to stay and accomplish his pilgrimage which he had vowed, and some besought him to return home. And while he doubted in his mind whether to tarry or to return, King Henry and the French prepared to march from Acre to besiege the fort of Darum. Then King Richard, leaving men to guard Ascalon, hastened with his own soldiers to Darum; and when the Turks saw such a small company they scorned them, and challenged them to come and fight with them. But the engines having arrived in the ship, were disjointed, and the King and his nobles carried them on their own shoulders from the shore, and, putting them together, set men to work them, and one of them the King managed himself, and by his command they threw stones at the city day and night.

Now Darum was very strongly built, with seventeen towers, one of which was stronger and higher than the others; and while the engines cast stones at the walls the King caused a mine to be made under the towers, and the slingers shot so well that none dared show themselves on the walls to do injury to the Christians. Then a tower fell down with a horrible noise, and the Christians rushed into the fort, slaughtering all the Turks who fell into their hands. Those who escaped fled for safety into the principal tower. Then the Christians set up their standards on the wall and threw down the banners of the Turks. But those who had fled to the tower, seeing that there was no succour for them, came out and gave themselves up to King Richard; and thus the fort of Darum was taken in four days, before the French could get to the place. And when King Henry was come King Richard gave it to him as the first-fruits of his kingdom.

And there came again a messenger from England named John de Alençon, and told the King how his brother Earl John was disturbing all the land of England. But the leaders of the Christian army—French, Norman, English, Poitevin, and Angevin—met together and bound themselves to go up to Jerusalem. And the King was much disturbed, and could not rest for care and anxiety; but while he doubted in his mind what to do a chaplain from Poitou, by name William, came to him as he sat in his tent troubled and perplexed, and prayed him with tears to remember all the great things he had done, and not now to sully his great name by forsaking the army at this time. And the King listened to him, and caused it to be proclaimed throughout the camp that he would not leave the Holy Land before Easter. And the soldiers rejoiced greatly, and, with great gladness, prepared to march up to Jerusalem.

And they came to Hebron, and were beset by swarms of little insects like sparks of fire, which troubled them much; for their sting was venomous, and the faces and hands of the pilgrims were swollen and so discoloured that they looked like lepers, and they were forced to cover themselves with veils, and in another place two men were bitten by serpents and died. But the men were full of courage, and counted their troubles but light, so that they might go up to Jerusalem, and the rich helped the poor, and gave them horses to ride on.

And they came to Betenoble, and tarried there for King Henry, who had gone to assemble the slothful who stayed behind at Acre. And while they dwelt there King Richard rode out to seek some Turks who were lying in ambush in the mountains, and he found them at the fountain of Emmaus, and put them to flight, killing twenty of them, and capturing the herald of Saladin and some horses, and camels, and mules. And as he was pursuing them he looked up, and beheld the city of Jerusalem.

But while the King was gone out of the camp there came down upon the French tents a company of two hundred Turks; and when the French, with the Templars and Hospitallers, went out to fight them, they would not fight on the plain, but rode up into the mountain. And the Christians pursued them, and one Robert de Bruges, an Hospitaller, rode into the ranks of the Turks all alone and ran his lance through the body of a Turk that it came out at his back. But he transgressed the rule of his order. Then the battle went on, and the French, wearied, began to give way, but the Count of Perche and the Bishop of Salisbury came quickly to their aid.

And there came from Joppa a caravan with provisions for the army under the care of Ferric of Vienna, and Baldwin de Carron, and Clarenbald de Mont Chablon; but on its way the people dispersed, and some of them tarried behind. Then there came upon them, not far from Ramleh, a company of Turkish horse, and a fierce fight began. Baldwin de Carron fought bravely and his companions. He was twice thrown from his horse, and mounted again; but Clarenbald forsook him and fled, and some of his men were slain. Then a third time he was brought to the ground and beaten with clubs till the blood flowed fast, and his sword was blunted and broken, and a knight who came to his aid was thrown down and mangled; and they would all have perished had not the Earl of Leicester come with great speed to their aid. And thus the Turks were driven off, and the wounded carried to the camp.

Then the people cried out to be led to Jerusalem, but King Richard and the leaders took counsel together, fearing the hazard was too great. And twenty men were chosen—French and Syrians, and Templars and Hospitallers; and the matter was laid before them. And tidings were brought to the King that there were caravans coming with great riches from Babylon. And King Richard, with a thousand men, and the Duke of Burgundy, with five hundred soldiers well armed, set out by night, and, marching by the light of the moon, came to the place. But Saladin was told by a spy of the King's setting forth, and he sent two thousand horsemen, with some foot-soldiers, to defend the caravan. Then the King, being led by his spies, came in sight at dawn of day, but they made haste to escape. So he fell upon them in two companies, and they could not stand before him, but fled before him like hares before the hounds, and left the caravan in their hands. And the King, mounted on a tall horse, riding first, pursued them far over the mountains; but some of them, turning aside, returned by another way and attacked our men, and thus the battle began again; but the Turks were slain in great numbers, and the ground was strewn with the dead. And when the battle was over the soldiers had great trouble in gathering together the camels and dromedaries, for they fled with great speed before the horses; but at last about four thousand seven hundred camels were taken, and mules and asses without number, besides a quantity of gold and silver, rich spices, silk clothes, and costly garments, with coats-of-mail, and arms and weapons, and a great store of tents and provisions of all kinds. Then they returned with their spoil to the camp, and King Richard, imitating the great King David, gave an equal share to the soldiers who had stayed in the camp. Thus they were provided with great store of beasts of burden ; but some of the young camels they killed, and roasting the flesh with lard, found it white meat and pleasant eating.

And the twenty counsellors dissuaded the King from going up to the siege of Jerusalem, for they said the summer was come, and there was great scarcity of water, for the Turks had blocked up the cisterns. But the people were filled with anger, and the French separated themselves from the army, and insulted King Richard, and the Duke of Burgundy wrote a scoffing song upon him. And thus disputing and quarrelling, the camp was broken up, and they returned to Joppa. Then King Richard destroyed the fort of Darum and strengthened the walls of Ascalon. And the army returned to Acre.

How Saladin came against Joppa, and of the admirable deeds of King Richard.

But Saladin, filled with joy at the departure of the King and his army, assembled all whom he could gather together, and he had twenty thousand horse-soldiers, and foot-soldiers innumerable. And they came down like locusts, and assaulted the town of Joppa. And the assault was so fierce that one of the gates was broken open, and the Turks entered the town, but the Christians fled into the fortress. And after they had defended the tower for a whole day the patriarch prayed Saladin to grant them a respite until the next day, and that then, if they did not receive assistance, they would give up the tower and pay a ransom for their lives. And to this he agreed, and took the patriarch and other chief men and bound them in chains as hostages.

But the people of Joppa had sent to King Richard for help, and when he heard of their danger he came with all the speed he could by ship to Joppa, but a contrary wind delayed him. Then the people, despairing of help, began to come out of the town, but as they came out and paid the money the Turks cut off their heads. Thus seven of them had died when the King's ships came sailing into the harbour.

Then the Turks came to the water and covered all the shore, and prepared to hinder the King from landing. But when the King perceived that he was yet in time to save the lives of some, he sprang into the water, and, with his men after him, gained the land, driving the enemy with shots from an arbalest, and then, drawing his sword, he cleared a path for himself, and forced a way into the city, which he entered first, and found three thousand Turks spoiling the tower. Then the Christians in the tower, when they saw the King, issued forth, and the town was filled with the dead bodies of the Turks. And Saladin, when he heard of the King's coming, left off to besiege the place, and the King began to repair the walls.

But in the Turkish army some evil men, called Menelones and Cordivi, being filled with shame that so small an army, without horses, should have put them to flight, and driven them forth from Joppa, made an agreement together that they would seize King Richard in his tent and bring him prisoner to Saladin. Therefore they armed themselves, and stealing forth by night came by the light of the moon to the camp while all lay asleep. Then the Cordivi said to the Menelones, 'Go in to the camp on foot, and take the King, while we remain here on horseback to hinder his escape.' But the Menelones answered, 'Nay, we are of higher rank than you, neither will we serve on foot; go ye in on foot, and we will tarry here.' Thus they tarried disputing until the dawn of day appeared, and a certain Genoese coming out of the camp early in the morning perceived the enemy and cried aloud, 'To arms! to arms!' The King, awakening, put on his coat of mail in haste and summoned his men, and they, catching up what armour and clothes they could, ran together. There were but ten knights besides the King, and some of their horses were unused to arms, but the King ordered the rest of the army skilfully, and the soldiers prepared to meet the fierce attack of the assailing Turks by kneeling with the right knee on the ground, covering themselves with their shields while their lances grasped in their hands rested with one end on the ground, and pointed their iron heads at the enemy. And between every two of these armed men the King placed an arbalester to annoy the enemy, and behind him waited another to load his arbalest. Thus the King ordered all as the short time allowed, and encouraged his men.

Then the enemy fell upon them in seven companies,

each having about one thousand horsemen. But they could not break through, for the Christians remained unmoved, and their lances were a wall unto them. And as the Turks fell back from the attack the cross-bowmen shot upon them, killing many of them. But many times the Turks rode against them like a whirlwind, and were forced to turn aside. Then the King, perceiving this, rode upon them with his knights, and broke through them, overthrowing them right and left, and not drawing rein till they had ridden quite through the Turkish army. The Earl of Leicester was flung from his horse, but the King came to his rescue, and helped him to remount. Sir Ralph de Mauleon was also seized and made prisoner, but the King spurred his horse and came upon the Turks who had hold of him, and forced them to yield him up. Where the fight was fiercest there rode the King, and the Turks fell beneath his flashing sword.

In the hottest of the battle there rode to the King a Turk, bringing with him two noble horses as a gift from the great Saphadin, Saladin's brother, for he knew that the King had sore need of horses, and he was a worthy foe.

Then the galley-men, fearing for their lives, left the battle, and took refuge in their boats, and the Turks thought to seize the town while the army was fighting in the field. But the King, taking with him but two knights and two cross-bowmen, entered the town, and dispersed the Turks who had entered, and set sentinels to guard it, and then, hasting to the galleys, gathered together the men, and, encouraging them with his words, brought them back to the fight. And as he led them to the field he fell upon the enemy so fiercely that he cut his way all alone into the midst of the ranks, and they gave way before them. But they closed around him, and he was left alone, and at that sight our men feared greatly. But alone, in the midst of his enemies, he remained unmoved, and all as they approached him were cut down like corn before the sickle. And there rode against him a great admiral, distinguished above the rest by his rich caparisons, and with bold arrogance essayed to attack him, but the King, with one blow of his sword, cut off his head, and shoulder, and right arm. Then the Turks fled in terror at the sight, and the King returned to his men, and lo! the King was stuck all over with javelins, like the spines of a hedgehog, and the trappings of his horse with arrows. The battle lasted that day from the rising to the setting sun, but the Turks returned to Saladin, and he mocked his men, and asked them where was Melech Ric, whom they had promised to bring him. But one of them answered, 'There is no knight on earth like Melech Ric, nay, nor ever was, from the beginning of the world.'

How the King fell sick, and how he made peace with Saladin for three years, and set forth to return into his own land.

But after the battle the King fell sick, and desired to go to Acre to be cured of his sickness, and he prayed the French, and the Templars, and the Hospitallers, to defend Ascalon and Joppa, but they all forsook him, and would give him no aid. Then the King, despairing of recovery, sought to negotiate a truce with Saladin. And he prayed Saphadin to mediate between them. And Saphadin, who honoured the King greatly, wrought with zeal on his behalf, and peace was made between them. And these were the terms of the peace: that Ascalon should be destroyed and not rebuilt for three years, and that the Christians should have Joppa and should go up to Jerusalem to the Holy Sepulchre without let or hindrance. And this peace should last for three years, until Richard, having returned to his own land, should have gathered a new army, and should come again to conquer the Holy Land. Then the King, remembering how the French had forsaken him, prayed Saladin not to give leave to any to visit the Holy Sepulchre except they came with letters from himself or Count Henry. Then the French, much disturbed in mind, returned to their own country, but as soon as they were departed King Richard caused it to be proclaimed that whoever wished might go up to the Sepulchre of our Lord.

Then the people made ready and went up in three companies to Jerusalem. And the first company was led by Andrew de Chamgui, and the second by Ralph Teissun, and the third by Hubert Walter, bishop of Salisbury, and Saladin received the bishop with great honour, and bade him make request for what he would and he would grant it. And he prayed for leave to place two Latin priests in Jerusalem, two at Bethlehem, and two at Nazareth, and the Sultan gave consent.

Then the pilgrims returned to Acre, and, taking ship, set sail for their own lands. But many perished by sickness or by shipwreck, and never returned to their homes.

Then the King prepared his ship, but before he departed he redeemed from captivity the brave William de Pratelles, who had given himself up for the King, and he gave in exchange for him ten noble Turks. And as the King departed the people lamented aloud, and blessed and praised the King, crying, 'Who will now defend thee, O Jerusalem, when King Richard is departed?' And all night the ship sailed by the light of the stars; and as morning dawned the King looked back towards the land and prayed aloud, saying, 'O Holy Land, I commend thee to God, and if in His mercy He grant me life, I hope to come yet again, and in His good pleasure to succour thee.' So spake he, not knowing the troubles and sorrows that awaited him.

CHAPTER V.

FULK FITZWARINE.

How Guarin of Metz won the love of Melette of the White Tower.

Now in the days when Owen Gwynned was Prince of Wales all the marches from Chester to Mount Gilbert lay waste and desolate, so cruelly did he ravage all the country round his land. The King of England, therefore, being wise, gave the lands of the marches to the most valiant knights in his army, that they should defend the march to their own profit and to the honour of their lord the King. Alberbury, with all the honour appertaining to it, he gave to a knight born in Lorraine, in the city of Metz, who was greatly renowned for his strength, beauty, and courtesy. His banner was of vermilion samite, with two gold peacocks. And the White Land, with its forests and chace, he gave to Payn Peverel, who died soon after in his castle in the Peak, and William Peverel, his sister's son, became his heir. He conquered much land, and built himself a tower, which he named the White Tower, and the town which is built round it is still called Whittington.

Now William had two fair nieces, Eleyne, the elder, and Melette, the younger, and he married Eleyne to Fitz-Alan, and gave her at her marriage all the land of Morlas. But Melette was most beautiful, and many desired her in marriage, but no one could please her, for she said, 'There is no knight in the world whom I will marry for his riches and his lands, but he must be handsome, courteous, and accomplished, and the most valiant knight in Christendom.' So William made a proclamation in many lands and many cities that all knights who were ready to joust for love should come to Castle Peverel, in the Peak, at the feast of St. Michael, and that the knight who should conquer should win the love of Melette of the White Tower, and become lord of Whittington and all its honours.

Now the brave Guarin of Metz had neither wife nor child, and he sent to John, duke of Little Britain, and prayed his aid and help in this matter; and the Duke had ten sons, the most valiant knights in all Little Britain,—Roger, the eldest, Howel, Audwyn, Urien, Thebaud, Bertrem, Amys, Gwychard, Gyrard, and Guy. So the Duke sent his ten sons and a hundred knights, well mounted and richly apparelled to his cousin Guarin of Metz. And there came to the tournament Eneas, the son of the King of Scotland, with the Earl of Moray, and the Bruces, Dunbars, Umfravilles, and two hundred knights, and Owen, Prince of Wales, with two hundred shields, and the Duke of Burgundy with three hundred; Ydromor, son of the King of Galloway, came with one hundred

RIDING TO THE TOURNAMENT

and fifty knights; and the knights of England were numbered at three hundred.

Guarin de Metz and his company lodged in tents in the forest near, and they were clothed in red samite, and their horses were covered with cloths that reached to the ground. Guarin himself, that he might be known from the others, had a crest of gold. Then sounded the drums, and trumpets, and Saracen horns, until the valleys re-echoed, and the tournament began.

Many a hard blow was given and many a knight thrown from his horse. The damsel, with other ladies, was in a tower watching the knights to see how each one bore himself; but the first day Guarin and his company were found to be the best and the most valiant, and among them Guarin was the most praised. When night came, Guarin and his company went back to their tents in the forest, and none of the other knights knew who they were. And the next day Guarin came to the jousts with a crest of green ivy out of the forest, like an unknown adventurer; and the Duke of Burgundy rushed upon him and struck him a great blow with his lance, but Guarin flung him from his horse, and a second, and a third. Then Melette of the White Tower sent him her glove and bade him fight for her. And he returned to the forest and put on his red armour, and came back with his companions and held the field against all comers; and he was declared the victor, and was adjudged the prize and Melette of the White Tower. So they sent for the bishop of the country, and he married them. And William Peverel gave a great feast; and when it was over, Guarin took his wife and went to Whittington. And the ten brothers and their knights prepared to return to Little Britain; but the youngest son, Guy, stayed behind in England, and he was called Guy L'Estrange; and from him are descended the great lords of that name.

Guarin de Metz held Whittington and defended it against the Welshmen. And he had a little son, named Fulk; and when he was seven years old he was sent to a famous knight, Joce de Dynan, to be taught the manners of chivalry.

How Fulk FitzWarine saved the life of Sir Joce de Dynan.

Now when Fulk was eighteen years old, tall and strong, Sir Joce went up to his tower early in the morning, and saw the fields covered with knights and squires, and among them he saw the banner of his great enemy, Sir Walter Lacy. So he bade his knights arm and mount their horses, and go down and guard the bridge; and they held it until Sir Joce came with five hundred men—knights and servants, and the citizens of the town of Dynan—with his banners, argent with three lions passant in azure, crowned with gold. He forced the bridge, and Lacy was discomfited and lost his banner and fled. But Joce de Dynan knew Walter de Lacy by his arms and saw him fleeing alone, so he put spurs to his horse and overtook Lacy in the wood near Bromfield, and called to him to turn. And when Lacy saw that Sir Joce was alone, he turned, and they fought long and many hard blows were given and taken. Joce struck Lacy through the shield and wounded his left arm, and would have taken him prisoner, but Sir Godard de Bruce and two knights came up to his aid and assaulted Sir Joce on all sides, but he defended himself like a lion.

Now Sir Joce's wife and his two daughters had climbed up into the tower to see the fight and to pray to God to guard their lord; and when they saw him so surrounded with enemies, they set up a great cry, and Fulk FitzWarine heard them (for Sir Joce had left him in the castle, being still but a youth), and he came to them and asked Hawyse the younger daughter what ailed her that she cried so? 'Hold your tongue!' she said, 'you are little like your bold father, for you are a coward and always will be. Do you not see that my lord, who has nourished and cherished you, is in peril of death for lack of help, and you walk up and down in safety and do nothing to aid him?' Upon that he turned red with anger, and going from the tower in haste, clad himself in an old rusty hauberk that he found, and took a great Danish axe; then he went to the stable and found there a cart-horse, and mounting it went out by the postern and came to the field just as his lord had been plucked from off his horse and was about to be killed. But with a blow of his axe he cut in two the backbone of Godard de Bruce, who had hold of his lord, and helped him to remount; then he turned to Sir Andrew de

Preez, and struck him such a blow on his helmet that he split his head down to his teeth. And when Sir Arnold de Lys found he could not escape, he surrendered to Sir Joce, and Lacy was taken also.

As they returned to the castle, Sir Joce turned to him and said, 'Friend burgess, you are very brave and strong, and if you had not been here I should have been killed.' Then the boy answered, 'Sir, I am no burgess. Do you not know me? I am Fulk, your foster child!' 'Fair son,' quoth he, 'blessed be the day I took you home! a man never loses what he does for a brave man.'

So Sir Walter de Lacy and Sir Arnold de Lys were led prisoners to the castle; but in a short space, by the falsehood of a servant, they escaped and got safely away.

And Fulk, who was called Fulk the Brown, because he had so dark a skin, was married to Hawyse, and Sir Joce made him heir of half his land.

But Sir Walter de Lacy pondered how he might be revenged; and though the lords of England made him and Sir Joce swear to live in peace, he gathered many men together from Ireland and other places, and came upon Sir Joce's castle of Dynan, when Sir Joce and Fulk were away, and by treachery obtained entrance into it; and they burnt the town and made a great slaughter of the people, young and old, and set up his banner on the Pendover Tower.

Now when the news came to Sir Joce, he gathered together an army of seven thousand men, and he, and Sir Guarin, and Fulk the Brown, came and laid siege to the castle; but it was strong and the siege lasted long, and Sir Guarin fell ill. So he returned to Alberbury with only one squire, and there he died. Fulk the Brown, when his father was dead, went to Alberbury and took homage of his people, and then returned to Sir Joce.

How Fulk Fitz Warine lost Whittington.

Sir Walter de Lacy, fearing that the war would go against him, sent to the Prince of Wales for aid, and he came with an army of twenty thousand Welsh, Scotch, and Irish, burning the towns and plundering the people. Sir Joce and Fulk, though they fought like lions, were overcome, and Sir Joce was wounded and taken prisoner. When Fulk saw him led away, he was mad with anger, but he was sore wounded himself and could not help, so he made his escape from the battle; but his enemies seized his lands and took his constable prisoner.

Now at that time King Henry was sojourning at Gloucester, and Fulk, all wounded as he was, made his way to him, and told him all that had befallen him. And the King was very furious and swore he would be avenged on all such malefactors. He showed himself also gracious to Fulk, and had his wounds healed, and sent for his mother, Melette, and his wife, Hawyse, and they dwelt in the Queen's chambers. And at this time a little son was born to him, and his name also was called Fulk.

Then the King sent a letter to Sir Walter de Lacy

and commanded him, as he valued life and limb, to deliver up Sir Joce whom he held in prison wrongfully; and Sir Walter was afraid, and entreated Sir Joce and his knights honourably, and set them free. So he came to the King, and he promised him law and right; and then he went to Lambourne, and soon after died and was buried there.

And the King made Fulk constable of his army, and bade him take men and drive the Welshmen out of the march, for Jervard Droyndoun, the prince, had driven out all the barons, and had taken the march from Chester to Worcester. Sir Fulk fought a battle with him at Hereford, and won the field; but the war lasted for four years, until, at the request of the King of France, a love-day was set between the King and Jervard the prince, and they made accord. And the Prince gave up the lands that he had conquered, but for no money would he yield Whittington; so King Henry gave to Sir Fulk instead Alveston and the honours appertaining to it, and Whittington was given to Roger de Powis. Thus Sir Fulk was disinherited of Whittington, and Sir Walter de Lacy holds wrongfully the castle of Dynan; but the town was rebuilt and named Ludlow.

How Fulk the Younger angered Prince John, and how he, when he became king, refused Fulk justice.

Sir Fulk and Hawyse lived with the King many years, and they had five sons,—Fulk, William, Philip the Red, John, and Alan. King Henry had four sons,

—Henry, Richard Cœur de Lion, Geoffrey, who was Count of Little Britain, and John, who was all his life wicked, and quarrelsome, and envious. Young Fulk was brought up with the King's four sons, and was much loved by all of them except John, with whom he quarrelled often. And it happened one day that John and Fulk were all alone in a room, playing at chess. John took the chess-board and struck Fulk a great blow. Fulk, finding himself hurt, raised his foot and gave John such a kick in his stomach that his head flew against the wall, and he fell down and fainted. Fulk was much afraid, but he was glad that there was no one else in the room, and he rubbed John's ears and recovered him from his faint. The Prince went to the King and made a great complaint, but the King only answered, 'Hold your tongue! you are always quarrelling. If Fulk did anything to you, you certainly deserved it.' And he sent for his master and bade him give him a good beating for complaining. But John kept his anger in his heart, and could never forgive Fulk.

And when King Henry was dead, Fulk the Brown, FitzWarine, found favour with King Richard, and he made all his sons knights. Then young Fulk and his brothers went over the seas and travelled in many lands, and whenever they heard of tournament or jousts, they went to the place and won everywhere honour and fame. But Fulk the Brown fell sick and died, and King Richard sent letters to young Fulk to come back to England and receive his lands. And when King Richard went to the Holy Land he gave the march into the care of Sir Fulk, and Sir Fulk was in high honour all the days of Richard.

But when King Richard was dead, John was crowned king; and he came to visit the march, and sojourned at Castle Baldwin, which is now called Montgomery. And when Moris, the son of Roger de Powis, Lord of Whittington, heard that the King was there, he sent him a fine horse and a white gerfalcon. And the King made him of his council, and Keeper of the March. Then Moris prayed the King to confirm to him the honour of Whittington. The King knew well that it belonged rightfully to Sir Fulk, but he remembered the blow that Fulk had given him, so he gave the land to Moris and sealed the writing with his seal. And Moris promised to give him a hundred pounds of silver.

But a knight went and told Fulk what the King had done; and he and his four brothers came to the King and prayed that he would give them their lands, and they would pay him a hundred pounds. But the King answered, that he would hold to his word to Sir Moris, whoever might be offended. Then Sir Moris said to Sir Fulk, 'Sir Knight, you are a fool if you challenge my lands. If you say you have a right to Whittington, you lie; and I would prove it on your body, if we were not in the King's presence!' Upon that, Sir William, Fulk's brother, without another word, rushed forward and struck Sir Moris a blow in his face with his fist. But the knights around interfered, and no more harm was done.

Then Sir Fulk turned to the King and said, 'Sir

King, you are my liege lord, and I am bound to you by fealty, as long as I am in your service, and hold my lands from you, and you ought to maintain my right; but you fail me in right and in common law. And it is no good king who denies to his tenant the law in his court; and, therefore, I give you back my homage.' And he turned and went away.

Then he and his brothers, and his cousin Baldwin de Hodnet, armed themselves; and when they were about half a league from the town, there came after them fifteen knights well armed, and commanded them to return, saying that they had promised to bring the King their heads. 'Fair sirs,' said Sir Fulk, 'you were fools to promise to give what you cannot get.' And they fought together; and four of the King's knights were killed, and all the others grievously wounded, except one who took to flight. And he came and told the King; and when the King saw how his knights were wounded he swore he would revenge them.

Sir Fulk went to Alberbury, and told his mother, Dame Hawyse, what had happened. And she gave him treasure; and he and his brothers went over the seas to Little Britain and sojourned there. But King John took all his lands, and did great injury to all his people.

How Sir Fulk and his brothers hid in the woods, and how the King appointed a hundred knights to take them.

Then, after a time, Sir Fulk and his brothers, and his cousins Baldwin de Hodnet and Aldulf de Bracy.

came back secretly to England. And they travelled at night, and by day hid themselves in the woods. But when they came to Alberbury, the people told them that their mother was dead; and Sir Fulk was much grieved, and prayed piteously for her soul.

And he and his people went to a forest called Babbing, near Whittington, to spy Moris Fitz-Roger. But a servant of Sir Moris saw them and told his master. Then Sir Moris armed himself and took his shield, which was green, with two boars or, the bordure was silver, with fleurs-de-lys in azure. And he had with him thirty men, well mounted, and five hundred on foot. But when Fulk saw him, he came out of the forest in haste, and a fierce fight began. And many were killed, and Sir Moris was wounded in the shoulder. At last Sir Moris fled towards the castle, and Fulk pursued him, and aimed a blow at his helmet, but it fell on the crupper of his horse; and Sir Fulk himself was wounded in the leg by an arrow from the castle. So Sir Moris escaped into the castle, and sent word to the King that Sir Fulk was returned to England.

Then the King appointed a hundred knights to go with their men through the land of England, and bring Sir Fulk to him alive or dead; and the King promised them great rewards of lands and money. So the knights rode about England; but when they heard he was in a place, they rode another way, for some of them loved him much, and others feared him for his strength and boldness.

Sir Fulk and his company came to the Forest of

Bradene; and there came by ten merchants with rich cloths, furs, and gloves for the King and Queen of England, and there were with them twenty-four soldiers to guard the King's treasure. When Fulk saw them, he sent his brother John to them to demand who they were and whence they came. But one of them demanded fiercely who he was that he should ask such a question. Then John asked them if they would come quietly to speak to his lord, for if they would not, he would make them. Upon that, one of the soldiers struck him a blow with his sword; but John felled him to the ground. Then Sir Fulk and his men came up and assailed the merchants. They defended themselves vigorously, but at last they were taken and carried into the forest. Then they told Sir Fulk that they were the King's merchants; at which Sir Fulk was very glad. And he said, 'Master Merchants, if you lose these goods who will suffer loss? Tell me truly.'

'Sir,' they answered; 'if we lose them by our cowardice or carelessness, we should suffer; but if we lose them by peril of sea or force of men, the loss would be the King's.'

When Sir Fulk heard that, he made them measure off the rich cloth and furs on his lance; and clothed all those that were with him, little and great, and every one had good measure. When evening was come, and the merchants had supped, he sent them away, and bade them carry to the King Fulk Fitz-Warine's salutations, and his thanks for his good cloths. Now Sir Fulk, all the time he was outlawed, never did harm to any one but the King and his knights.

And when the King heard from the merchants and soldiers what had happened to them, he was mad with rage. And he sent a proclamation through his kingdom that whosoever would bring him Fulk, alive or dead, he would give him a thousand pounds of silver and all the lands that belonged to Fulk in England.

Then Fulk went into the forest of Kent, and, leaving his knights in the forest, went riding alone on the highroad; and he met a messenger coming along singing, with a chaplet of red roses on his head. And Sir Fulk asked to give him the chaplet, and he would pay him double what it was worth. But the man answered, 'Sir, he must be very niggardly of his goods who will not give a chaplet of roses to a knight.' So he gave the chaplet to Fulk, and Sir Fulk gave him twenty sous for it.

Now the man knew him well, for he had often seen him; and he came to Canterbury, and met there the hundred knights who had sought Fulk through England. And he asked them what they would give him if he led them to the place where he was. And they promised so much that he told them how he had met him and given him the chaplet. Then the hundred knights summoned all the knights, and squires, and soldiers, and raised the country, and besieged the forest; and they sent people to start the game, as if they had been hunting, and people with horns to tell them when Sir Fulk and his companions came out of the forest.

And when Sir Fulk heard the sound of a bugle he divined what had happened, and he, and his brothers, and cousins, and all his men, mounted and issued from the forest; and they came upon the hundred knights, and charged them, and killed some of them, and passed through them. But when he saw that behind them were knights, and squires, and burgesses, and people without number, he knew that he was not able to fight them all, and they returned to the forest; but John was wounded in the head. The people pursued them a long way, but at last they escaped; and, leaving their horses behind them, fled on foot to an abbey that was near. The porter seeing them ran to lock the gates; but Alan, who was very tall, leaped over the walls, and seizing the porter, took the keys from him, and let the others in.

Then Fulk put on the habit of an old monk, and took a great stick in his hand and went out, and made them shut the gate after him. He went, leaning on his staff and limping as if he were very lame. And the knights, and the soldiers, and a great crowd of people, overtook him.

And a knight cried to him, 'Old monk! have you seen any armed knights pass this way?'

'Yes, sir, and may they be punished for the evil they have done!'

'Why? What have they done to you?'

'Sir,' he said, 'I am old and infirm, and can no longer help myself; and there came seven on horses, and fifteen on foot, and because I could not clear the road quickly, they made their horses ride over me.'

'You shall be soon avenged,' said he. And they rode on in haste to overtake Fulk, and were soon a league from the abbey.

After they were gone, came Sir Girard de Malfée and his companions, well mounted on costly horses, for they had come from abroad. And Sir Girard looked on him and said, mockingly, ' Here is a fine fat monk, big enough to hold two gallons!' Now Fulk's brothers were watching inside the gate. And Fulk, without a word, raised his stick and struck Sir Girard behind the ear and he fell to the ground stunned. And Fulk's brothers, rushing out of the gate, took all the knights prisoners, and bound them in the porter's lodge, and took their armour and their horses, and never ceased riding till they came to Huggeford. And there they stayed till John was healed of his wound.

How Sir Fulk married Dame Maude de Caus, and slew a knight named Sir Piers de Bruville.

Now while they were there, there came to them a messenger, who had been seeking them a long time, with salutations from Hubert, archbishop of Canterbury, who prayed him to come in haste to speak with him. So Sir Fulk and his men returned to the forest near Canterbury; and he and his brother William disguised themselves as merchants, and came to the Archbishop, and he said to them, 'Fair sons, you are very welcome. You know that Sir Theobald Butler, my brother, had married Dame Maude de

Caus, a very rich lady, and the most beautiful in England. And now that he is dead, King John is trying to seize her and carry her away; and I have sent for you, Sir Fulk, to pray you to take her to wife.' And Sir Fulk saw her, and knew that she was fair and good, and had in Ireland many castles and lands, and with the assent of his brother William he was married to Dame Maude de Caus; and he stayed there two days, and then leaving his wife in the care of the Archbishop, he returned to the wood, and told his companions; and they asked him where the fine castle was to which he would take his wife, and made great game of him.

Now there was living in the marches of Scotland a knight named Robert Fitz-Sampson, who was rich, and would often receive Sir Fulk and give him lodging. And his wife, Dame Amable, was a very courteous lady. And in the same country was a knight, Piers de Bruville, who used to assemble the wild youths and ribald people and kill and rob the merchants and others. And he gave out that he was Fulk FitzWarine; so that Fulk and his companions had much blame for things that they had not done. Now Fulk, who could never stay long in one place, came by night to the house of Sir Robert Fitz-Sampson. And he made his companions wait outside, but seeing a great light, he went boldly into the hall, and Sir Piers de Bruville and his knights were sitting at supper. But Sir Robert Fitz-Sampson and his good lady and his servants were lying on the ground bound. Sir Piers and his knights wore masks,

I

but those who served him bent the knee to him and called him Sir Fulk. And the lady cried piteously, 'Ha! Sir Fulk, I have never done you any harm, but have always loved you.' Then Sir Fulk, when he heard that, could be silent no longer, but, all alone as he was, stepped forward, with his sword drawn in his hand, and swearing that if any one dared to move he would cut him into little pieces, demanded which of them called himself Fulk. 'Sir,' said Piers, 'I am a knight, and am called Fulk.' 'Then, Sir Fulk,' he answered, 'get up at once and bind all your companions, or you shall be the first to lose your head.' And Piers, terrified at the menace, rose and unbound the lords, lady, and all the servants of the house, and bound his companions. Then Sir Fulk made him cut off all their heads, and when that was done he himself cut off the head of Sir Piers, saying, 'I will pay you that you have deserved for bringing upon me the charge of robbery.'

Then Sir Fulk left the marches of Scotland, and returned to a forest near Alberbury; for though he was so bold, he was too wise to remain long in one place, for the King's people were ever in pursuit of him, and sometimes, to deceive them, he would have his horses shod with their shoes reversed. One of Sir Fulk's men was a clever minstrel and juggler, and his name was John de Rampaigne; and Sir Fulk sent him to Whittington to spy upon Moris Fitz-Roger. So he took a certain herb, and crushed it, and put it in his mouth, and his face began to swell, and became so discoloured that his companions even hardly knew him. Then he dressed himself in poor clothes, and took his box of juggler's tools and a great stick, and went to Whittington, and told the porter he was a juggler. Then the porter took him in to Sir Moris Fitz-Roger, and Moris asked him of what country he was. And he answered that he was born in the march of Scotland. Then Sir Moris asked what news he brought; and he answered that he had none, except that Sir Fulk FitzWarine had been killed while robbing the house of Sir Robert Fitz-Sampson.

'Is that true?' cried Sir Moris.

'Certainly,' he replied; 'all the people of the country say so.'

'Minstrel,' answered he, 'for your news I will give you this cup of fine silver.'

So the minstrel took the cup and gave him many thanks.

Now John was an ugly, clumsy fellow, and the household servants mocked him, and pulled his hair, and treated him roughly. But he, enraged, struck one of them on the head with his stick, and knocked out his brains. Then Sir Moris swore that, but for the news he had brought, he would have had his head cut off. So the juggler made haste to escape; and he returned to Sir Fulk, and told him that he had heard say in the house that Sir Moris and his fifteen knights and attendants were going the next day to the castle of Shrewsbury, for he was keeper of the march.

Then Sir Fulk was glad, and the next morning he and his companions armed themselves and rode out of the forest. And Sir Moris and his knights came riding on the way to Shrewsbury, and he looked towards the pass of Nesse; and he saw coming a man with a shield quartered with gules and indented argent, and by the arms he knew it was Fulk. 'Now know I,' said Sir Moris, 'that jugglers are liars, for there is Fulk.' But Moris and his companions were bold knights, and they attacked Sir Fulk and his men, calling them thieves, and crying that their heads should be on the high tower of Shrewsbury before the evening. But Sir Fulk and his men defended themselves well, and Sir Moris and his fifteen knights and his companions were slain; so Sir Fulk had so many fewer enemies.

How Sir Fulk went to the Prince of Wales.

Then Sir Fulk passed over to Rhuddlan to Sir Lewis, Prince of Wales, for the Prince had been brought up with Sir Fulk at King Henry's court. And the Prince received him gladly, and asked him how he and the King were accorded. 'Not at all, sir,' answered Fulk. 'I cannot have peace for anything, and therefore I have come to you.' 'Certainly,' said the Prince, 'I will give you my peace. The King of England will have peace neither with you, nor me, nor any one else.' So Sir Fulk thanked him; and then he told him that Sir Moris Fitz-Roger was dead, for he had killed him. Now Sir Moris was the Prince's cousin, and he was much enraged, and said if he had not given him his peace he would have had him drawn and hanged. But the Princess Joan came and made accord between them, and they kissed each other.

Prince Lewis ordered Sir Fulk to march against his enemy Gwenwynwyn, and to ravage his land; but Sir Fulk knew that it was the Prince who was to blame, and he reasoned with him, and the Prince listened to him, and made peace with Gwenwynwyn.

Then news came to King John at Winchester that Sir Fulk had killed Sir Moris, and was now living with Prince Lewis, who had married Joan of England. He became very pensive, and fell into a long silence. Then he said, 'Ha, St. Mary! I am King of England, Duke of Anjou and Normandy, and Lord of all Ireland, and yet I cannot find any one who will avenge me of the damage and shame that Fulk has done me. But I will not fail to avenge myself of the Prince.' So he summoned to Shrewsbury all his earls and barons and knights.

And Prince Lewis was warned that the King was preparing for war, and he called Sir Fulk and told him. Then Sir Fulk assembled an army of thirty thousand men at Castle Balaham in Pentlyn, and Gwenwynwyn and his men came too. Sir Fulk was skilful in war, and knew all the passes by which King John could enter. And there was a very narrow pass called the Ford of Gymele, shut in by woods and marshes, so that it could only be traversed by the high-road. Then Fulk and Gwenwynwyn dug a deep and wide ditch across the highway, and filled it with water, and made a palisade behind it. The ditch may still be seen.

So King John and his army came to the place and found ten thousand knights guarding the passage. But Fulk and his companions, with Gwenwynwyn and several other knights, had crossed by a secret path, and were on the same side as the King. And a fierce skirmish began, Fulk and his men fighting like lions, and killing many of the King's knights, and being often dismounted themselves. But Gwenwynwyn was sore wounded in the head; so Fulk and his men returned by the secret path and defended the ditch, and the fight lasted, with great loss to the King, until evening, when he returned to Shrewsbury.

Then the Prince gave back to Sir Fulk his inheritance of Whittington, and the knight was very glad, and had it repaired. And he gave a great feast because he had a new entry into his land, and there came to him seven hundred knights from Wales and many others. But the King sent against him Sir Henry de Audley and Sir John Lestrange, whose castle had been destroyed by Prince Lewis; and they came with ten thousand knights, killing all they met, both men and women, and robbing the country. So Sir Fulk and his friends went out to meet them. And when Sir John saw Sir Fulk he spurred his horse and charged Sir Fulk with his lance so fiercely that it flew into little pieces. But Sir Fulk struck Sir John through his helmet, so that he kept the mark in his face all his life, and he fell flat on the ground. But he was a valiant man, and sprang to his feet, and cried aloud, 'Now, lords, all at Fulk!' And Fulk answered proudly, 'Right! and Fulk at all!'

And the battle grew fierce, and Sir Fulk and his men killed many knights, but Alan and Philip Fitz-Warine were wounded. And when Sir Fulk saw that, in his rage he pushed into the thick of the fight. But he had but seven hundred knights, and the others were ten thousand and more; so he was forced to return to Whittington. Sir Audulf de Bracy was dismounted, and, though he defended himself bravely, he was at last taken and led prisoner to Shrewsbury. Sir Henry and Sir John were proud of their prize, and they brought him to the King, who swore that he would have him drawn and hanged, because he was a traitor and a thief. But to that Sir Audulf replied that he was no traitor, nor any of his lineage.

Of Sir Audulf de Bracy and John de Rampaigne.

Now Sir Fulk was at Whittington with his brothers and other wounded knights, but when he heard that Sir Audulf could not be found he made great lamentation. Then came John de Rampaigne and said, 'Leave this lamentation; if God please, I will bring you good news of him to-morrow.' Now he was skilled in the tabor and harp, and he dressed himself richly, as if he had been a baron. And he dyed his hair and all his body as black as jet, so that there was nothing white about his body but his teeth. And he hung a tabor round his neck, and mounted a fine palfrey, and rode through the town of Shrewsbury to the gate of the castle. And he came to the King, and knelt before him, and saluted him. The

King asked him whence he came. 'Sir,' he answered, 'I am an Ethiopian minstrel, born in Ethiopia.'

'Then,' said the King, 'are all the people of your land of your colour?'

'Yea, my lord; both man and woman.'

'And what do they say of me in those strange lands?'

'Sir,' he answered, 'you are the most renowned king in all Christendom; and because of your renown have I come to see you.'

'Welcome, fair sir,' answered the King.

Then John said he was more renowned for wickedness than goodness, but that the King did not hear.

So that day John showed his minstrelsy, and played before the King on his tabor and other instruments. And when the King was gone to bed Sir Henry de Audley sent for the black minstrel, and brought him to his chamber; and he played before him. And when Sir Henry had drunk well, he said to his servant, 'Go and fetch Sir Audulf de Bracy, whom the King will have killed to-morrow. Let him have a good night before his death.' So he was brought into the room, and they talked and played. Then John began a song that Sir Audulf used to sing, and he raised his head and looked him in the face, and, with great trouble, recognised him.

Then Sir Henry called for wine, and John was very serviceable, and sprang to his feet, and handed the cup before any one else could reach it. But John put a powder in the cup, and no one saw him, for he was a good juggler, and all who drank became sleepy. And when they were all asleep John took one of the King's fools, and put him between the two knights who were to guard Sir Audulf. Then Sir Audulf and John took all the linen and towels in the room, and escaped by a window, and went away to Whittington, which was twelve leagues from Shrewsbury. And when Fulk rose early in the morning, for he could sleep little, he looked towards Shrewsbury and saw Sir Audulf and John coming. He ran to them and kissed them, and Sir Audulf told them of John's doings, and how they had escaped.

Now when the King heard that Sir Fulk had married Dame Maude de Caus, he did great damage to the Archbishop and the lady, and she took refuge in the minster. There she bore a little daughter, and the Archbishop baptized her Hawyse. She became afterwards lady of Wem. Then Fulk and his companions came by night to Canterbury, and took his wife to Huggeford, and afterwards she dwelt secretly at Alberbury. And when she found she was not safe there she fled to the church of Our Lady at Shrewsbury, and there she bore another daughter, who was baptized Joan, and who was afterwards married to Sir Henry de Pembridge. Afterwards Dame Maude had a son, who was born on a mountain in Wales, and was baptized by the name of John in a stream which comes out of the Maiden's Spring. But when the child was confirmed by the Bishop he was named Fulk.

Now when the King saw he could not prevail against Fulk, he wrote a letter to Prince Lewis, and said he would give him all the lands that his ancestors had ever taken if he would give him up the body of Fulk. But it was told Fulk what the King had said, and he sent away Dame Maude secretly to the care of the Bishop of Canterbury. And he and his brothers armed themselves and went to Prince Lewis, and told him he had had a letter and had not showed it to them. The Prince prayed him to stay, for he had not thought to betray him, but Fulk answered, 'Sir, I believe you well, but I will no longer stay.' So he took leave of him, and they travelled night and day and came to Dover and took ship, and arrived at Whitsand.

How Sir Fulk and his brothers went over the sea to the King of France.

Then they came to Paris, and King Philip was gone to the fields to watch his knights jousting. And when the Frenchmen saw the English knights stand by, one of them, Sir Druz de Montbener, sent to challenge Sir Fulk to joust with him. And Sir Fulk and his knights armed themselves and mounted their horses, and John de Rampaigne struck the tabor at the entry of the lists until the hills and valleys resounded and the horses danced with glee. When the King saw Sir Fulk in arms, he said to Sir Druz de Montbener, 'Think well what you do, for I perceive well this English knight is very valiant.' 'Sire,' he answered, 'there is not a knight on earth whom I dare not encounter on horse or on foot, body to body.' So Sir Fulk and Sir Druz spurred their horses, and met, and Sir Fulk's lance pierced through the shield, and the good hauberk, to his shoulder, and then flew to pieces, and Sir Druz fell to the ground. And Sir Fulk took Sir Druz's horse, and led it away, but he sent it back as a present to Sir Druz. Then came a French knight to avenge Sir Druz, and pierced Sir Fulk's shield, but Sir Fulk struck him on the helmet so that he left his saddle, whether he would or not.

Then the King rode up to Sir Fulk and bade him welcome, and prayed him to stay with him. And Fulk won everywhere much praise, and was ever the first where boldness, chivalry, prowess, or goodness, were to be found. So he dwelt with the King of France, but he told him not who he was, but called himself Amis du Bois. But when the King of England heard that Sir Fulk was dwelling with the King of France, he sent to pray the King that he would send away his mortal enemy, Fulk FitzWarine. Then the King of France replied that he had no such knight in his retinue. But Fulk came to the King and prayed for leave to depart. Then the King understood that he was Fulk FitzWarine, and he said, 'Stay with me, and I will give you richer lands than you ever had in England.'

'But,' answered Fulk, 'he is not worthy to receive lands by gift that cannot hold those that came to him by heritage.'

So he took leave of him, and came to the sea, and saw the ships afloat, and the weather was fine. And he called a sailor to him who seemed hardy and bold, and said, 'Is that ship yours?'

'Yes, sir,' answered he.

'What is your name?' and he said, 'Mador, of the Mount of Russia, where I was born.'

'Mador,' said Fulk, 'do you know your business well, and can you take people by sea into various regions?' and he answered, 'There is no land in Christendom which I do not know well.'

'Truly,' said Fulk, 'you have a perilous trade. Tell me by what death did your father die?'

Mador answered, 'He was drowned at sea.'

'And your grandfather?'

'He, too.'

'And your great-grandfather?'

'In the same way, and all my relations that I know of, to the fourth degree.'

'Then,' said Fulk, 'you are foolhardy to dare to go to sea.'

'Why, sir,' he answered, 'everyone dies the death to which he is destined; and, tell me, where did your father die?'

'In his bed, certainly.'

'And your grandfather and your great-grandfather?'

'In the same way, all of our lineage, that I know of, have died in their beds.'

'Then,' said Mador, 'I marvel greatly that you dare ever go to bed.'

Fulk then prayed Mador to prepare a ship at his expense, so a ship was made in a forest near the sea, with all the cordage that appertained to it, and prepared and victualled richly. Then Fulk and his bro-

thers put to sea, and ran along the coast of England.
And a well-armed ship approached them, and a knight
called to Mador and asked whose ship it was, and he
answered that it was his.

'Nay,' said the knight, 'on the sail are the arms
of Fulk FitzWarine, and he is on board, and this day
I will deliver him to King John.'

But Mador, who was a bold sailor, let his ship sail,
and it struck the other ship in the middle, and the sea
rushed in. But ere the ship foundered many a blow
was struck, and Fulk and his men captured great spoil.

Fulk coasted England a whole year, injuring none
but the King, and then he sailed away and visited
many lands—Gothland, Norway, Denmark, Orkney,
Ireland, and Scandinavia, and saw strange things and
had many perilous adventures, and fought with many
monsters and wild beasts.

How Sir Fulk took King John prisoner in the forest of Windsor.

Afterwards they sailed back to England, and
landed at Dover, and they heard that King John was
at Windsor. So they started for Windsor, travelling
by night and resting in the woods by day, and they
came to the forest of Windsor. And they heard the
sound of horns, and knew that the King was going
hunting. Then Fulk swore a great oath that nothing
should stop him from avenging himself on the King,
who wrongfully and by force had disinherited him,
and he made his companions stay behind, and went

out alone. And as he went he met an old charcoal-burner, carrying a sieve in his hand, and he had on black clothes fit for a charcoal-burner. Then Fulk prayed him to give him his clothes and his sieve, and he bought them for ten besants, and he sent the charcoal-burner away, and bade him tell no man. Then he dressed himself in the clothes and set himself to arrange the fire with a great iron fork. And while he was thus busy, there came by the King and three knights, all on foot. When Fulk saw the King he threw away his fork, and threw himself humbly on his knees, and the excellent breeding and carriage of the charcoal-burner caused great merriment to the King and his knights.

'Master villain,' said the King, ' have you seen any stag or doe pass this way?'

'Yes, my lord; a little while ago.'

'What sort of beast did you see?'

'One with long horns, my lord; and I could lead you to the place.'

'On, then, master villain, and we will follow.'

'Sir,' said the charcoal-burner, 'may I take my fork with me, for it would be a great loss to me if it were taken?'

So the King gave him leave, and Fulk took the great iron fork with him, and led the King into another part of the forest. Then he said, 'If it will please you, my lord, to wait here, I will go and drive the beast this way.' But he went quickly to his companions, and they all rushed out upon the King and seized him.

Then said Sir Fulk, 'Now, Sir King, I have you in my power, and will judge you as you would judge me if you had taken me.'

But the King, trembling for fear, cried him mercy, and promised he would give him back all his heritage, and all that he had taken from him, and would grant him his peace and love all his life. So Fulk made him pledge his faith before his knights and then let him go.

But the King returned to his palace and assembled his knights, and told them how Fulk had treated him, but that, as he had made him swear by force, he would not keep his oath, but bade them arm quickly, and go take those felons in the park. Then Sir James of Normandy, a cousin of the King's, begged to have the advanced guard. 'For all these English,' he said, 'are cousins of Sir Fulk, and traitors to the King, and will not take him.'

Then answered Randolf, Earl of Chester, 'Saving the honour of the King, not yours, you lie, for we are no traitors, though all the great men and the King himself are cousins of Sir Fulk.' And he would have struck him with his fist if the earl-marshal had not been there. Then Sir James of Normandy and his fifteen knights armed themselves in white armour, and mounted their white horses, and rode out in haste.

But Sir Fulk heard of these doings, for John de Rampaigne had spied out the matter, and he and his men went out to meet them, and killed many of them, and took Sir James prisoner. Then they armed themselves in the Normans' white armour, and mounted their white horses, for their own horses were tired, and they armed Sir James in Sir Fulk's armour, and bound his mouth so that he could not speak, and put his helmet on his head, and rode to the King. And they presented Sir James prisoner to the King, saying they had taken Sir Fulk, but they must ride away quickly and pursue the other FitzWarines. So the King dismounted from his horse, and gave it to Sir Fulk, and they rode away into the wood and washed and bound their wounds, for William was sore wounded, and they feared he would die.

Then the King commanded them to hang Sir Fulk; but when they took off his helmet, they found it was not Sir Fulk, but Sir James of Normandy. And when the King perceived that he had been deceived, he, with his earls and barons, followed the trace of the horses' feet and came to the place where Sir Fulk was making lamentation over his wounded brother. Then William begged that his brother would cut off his head and not let him fall into the hands of his enemies; but Fulk would not. And Randolf, Earl of Chester, came first to the spot, and sending back his men, went forward by himself and prayed Sir Fulk to yield himself to the King, and he would answer for him for life and limb. But Sir Fulk would not consent, but bade him go back to the King and do his duty in fighting against him; only he prayed him when his brother was dead, to care for his burial. Then Randolf returned to his men, and Fulk stayed weeping and praying by his brother.

Then the attack was made, and the Earl of Chester

WILLIAM FITZ WARINE WOUNDED

fought bravely, and Fulk and his men defended themselves well. But a knight came behind Sir Fulk and wounded him in the side and thought to have killed him. And Fulk turned, and holding his sword in both hands, struck him a blow on his left shoulder and cut down to his heart, so he fell dead; but the blood poured from Fulk's wound, and he fell fainting on his horse's neck, and his sword dropped from his hand. Then the brothers lamented sore, and his brother John sprang up behind him on his horse and held him up, and they all made haste to flee. The King and his men pursued, but could not overtake them. They fled all that night, and the next morning came to the sea and to Mador with the ship. Then Fulk awoke and asked where he was; and they made him a bed in the ship, and John de Rampaigne dressed his wounds.

How Sir William FitzWarine was rescued.

After the battle was over the Earl of Chester found William FitzWarine nigh death, and had him carried to an abbey to be doctored. But the matter was told the King, and he was much enraged against Earl Randolf, and commanded that William should be brought in a litter to Windsor and thrown into a deep dungeon. And the ship sailed away to Spain, and Fulk's wound healed; and they went to the land of Barbary, and made themselves famous everywhere by their prowess and knightly deeds.

Then they returned to England laden with riches

that the King of Barbary had given them. And
they desired much to learn whether their brother
William was in life or no. So John de Rampaigne
disguised himself as a merchant, and came to London,
and lodged in the house of the Mayor. Then he gave
many fair gifts to the household, and won favour with
the Mayor, and prayed him to obtain leave from the
King for his ship to come to shore. And he spoke
ever in corrupt Latin, but the Mayor understood him
well. And he brought him to the King at Westminster, and the King asked him who he was and
whence he came. 'Sir,' said he, 'I am a Greek merchant, and have been in Babylon, Alexandria, and
India the Greater, and my ship is laden with rich
cloths, pearls, and horses, and other valuable things.'
So the King gave him leave to bring his ship to
shore, and he commanded him to stay and eat; so
the Mayor and the merchant ate together before the
King. While they were eating there came in two
sergeants-at-mace, and brought in a tall knight with
a long, black beard, and made him sit down in the
hall, and brought him food. Then the merchant
asked the Mayor who he was, and he told him his
name was William FitzWarine; and he recounted to
him the doings of him and his brothers. Then John
was very glad to see he was still in life; and he went
back to Sir Fulk and told him of his brother, and
they brought the ship as near the city as they could.

The next day the merchant brought a white palfrey, the like of which could not be found in the
kingdom, and presented it to King John. And he

gave so largely to all that he became much beloved, and could do at court whatever he pleased.

Then one day he and his companions armed themselves, and then put on their mariners' gowns, and came thus to Westminster; and as they entered they met William FitzWarine going with his guard towards the prison. And they fell suddenly on his guard, and carried him away by force to their boat, which was floating near. The guard called for help; but the merchants defended themselves well, and escaped to their ship and sailed away.

How the King made peace with Sir Fulk and gave him back his lands, and how Sir Fulk died and was buried.

And they came to Little Britain, and stayed with their cousins there for half-a-year. But Fulk longed ever to be in England. So he returned, and they went to the New Forest; and as they wandered there they encountered the King pursuing a wild boar. And they seized him and six of his knights, and carried him away to their galley. There they had many words; but at last the King agreed to pardon them, and to give them back all their heritage, and that their peace should be cried through all England. And he left his six knights with them as hostages.

Then he went to Westminster and summoned all his earls, and barons, and clergy, and told them that he had granted his peace to Fulk FitzWarine, his brothers, and adherents, and had given them their heritage; and he commanded that they should be honourably received throughout the realm. When the Archbishop Hubert heard that, he was glad, and he sent letters to Fulk, and to the Earl of Gloucester, and Earl Randolf, and to Hugh, earl-marshal, to come to him at Canterbury; and when they were come they agreed that Fulk and his brothers should go at once to the King. So Fulk and his brothers, with the three earls, put on as rich attire as they could, and rode through London to the King at Westminster, and knelt before him, and yielded themselves to him. And the King received them graciously, and they dwelt with him a whole month. Then Fulk went and dwelt with the Earl Marshal, and he gave him Ashdown and Wantage; and Fulk made at Wantage a fair and a market town.

Then he took leave of the Earl Marshal and went to the Earl of Chester, who was arming his men to defend his rights in Ireland; and Fulk went with him and fought for him, and the Earl subdued all his lands.

So Fulk came back to Whittington, and Dame Maude and his children rejoiced greatly to see him. And he returned with great riches, and gave largely to his soldiers and friends, and maintained himself in great honour. And he was very hospitable, and turned the high-road through his hall at Alveston, that none might pass without meat and lodging. Then he bethought himself of all the blood that he had shed, and in remission of his sins he founded a priory near Alberbury, in a wood on the river Severn.

And not long after, Dame Maude de Caus, his wife, died, and was buried in this priory.

Then a good while after she was dead Fulk married a noble, sweet lady, Dame Clarice de Auberville, and they had many fair children.

And it came to pass one night that Fulk lay thinking of his youth and repenting of his sins, and he saw in the chamber a marvellously bright light, and heard a voice like thunder saying, 'Vassal, God has granted thee penance, for it is better here than elsewhere.' And his wife woke and saw the light, and hid her face for fear. And when the light was gone Fulk was found blind, and he remained blind all the rest of his days.

And Dame Clarice died, and was buried at the New Abbey; and Fulk lived but a year longer, and died at Whittington, and was buried at New Abbey with great honour.

CHAPTER VI.

PRINCE EDWARD AT THE LAST CRUSADE.

Now when the barons had been brought to submit to the King's mercy, and peace had been proclaimed throughout the kingdom, it came to pass that the Christians were stirred up against the Saracens, who long time had held possession of the sanctuary of the Lord; and by the diligence of Clement, the Roman pontiff, great numbers of Christian people assembled, and the most powerful princes took the holy sign. Among them was Edward, the King's son, and he set forth in the summer of the year 1270. Then about the feast of St. Michael he came to Aigue-mortes, which lies about eighteen leagues to the west of Marseilles, and there he took ship, and, sailing with a favourable wind, came on the tenth day to Tunis, where he was received with great joy by the Christian kings whom he found there—by Philip, of France, who had become king by the death of his father, St. Louis, not long before, by Charles, king of Sicily, and by the two kings of Navarre and Aragon. All these kings were assembled from zeal for God and Christ's people, and to them now came Edward for himself and his father and Henry, the son of the King of Germany, in the stead of his father. Now this Henry, on returning to his father, was slain at Viterbo in the chapel while he was hearing mass, by Guy de Montfort and Count Rufus, whose daughter Guy had married, in revenge for the death of Earl Simon.

And when Edward inquired of the kings concerning matters, they replied, 'The prince of this city and the surrounding country is bound to pay tribute every year to the King of Sicily, and because for seven years and more he had ceased to pay it we came upon him. But he, knowing that he ought justly to pay the tribute, has already satisfied our demands both for past and future times.'

To which he answered, 'What! my good lords, this manner of dealing becomes us not; we have assumed the sign of the Lord to go against the enemies of the Cross of Christ, and not to make agreements with them. Be it far from us! for the way is open and the land smooth and plain before us, that we may go up to the holy city, Jerusalem.'

But they answered, 'We have already concluded a peace, and it is not lawful for us to break it, but let us return into Sicily, and when the winter is past we can sail for Acre.'

And this counsel displeased him, neither would he give assent to the peace, nor take any part of the unlawful money, but held himself aloof from their royal feasts. But they, remaining fixed in their determination, when the wind blew, entered their ships. And there remained on the shore more than two hundred men, having no ships to sail in, crying out for fear of the death that they must shortly suffer if they were left behind. Then Edward, moved by their tears, though the others cared not for them, went to the shore with a boat, and making room in his several ships, sent them all before him, coming himself with the last; so they set sail and departed.

And on the seventh day they came to the kingdom of Sicily, opposite the city of Trapani, and on the day before the feast of St. Simon and St. Jude, about noon, they anchored in the high sea, more than a mile from shore, for they had large ships, each having two sails, and they were overloaded; and there came out to meet them from the port of the city many boats, which going backwards and forwards two or three times, carried to land the kings, and princes, and most of the soldiers, but few of the horses and almost none of the arms. Then towards evening the sea began to rise, and there was a great tempest, so that the ships, being dashed one against another, were broken, and there were lost more than a hundred and twenty, with the horses, and arms, and many men, and the unlawful treasure perished, and was swallowed up in the deep sea; but all the ships of Edward, in number about thirteen, were unharmed by the tempest, nor did a man of them perish, for the Lord saved them because he would not consent to their evil counsel.

Then, when the morning was come, and the kings came to the shore, and saw the bodies of the drowned men and the horses without number, they mourned, for out of so many ships and one thousand five hundred

sailors, besides the common people, there remained
none but the sailors of one ship, and that fell out in
this way. There was in that ship a good countess,
who, seeing the peril and fearing it justly, inquired of
the sailors whether they could be saved if they tried
to reach the shore. And they answered, ' What was
the good ? if the men were saved and the ship itself
were lost.' And she answered, ' Care not for the
ship, for if the lives are saved I will give you
double the price of the ship.' So, raising two sails,
they ran the ship far on to the land with such
force that it remained fixed, but the sailors, knowing that it was to be paid for twice over, they saved
all the people, to the joy of all. Thus the kings
came back to their lands, and their horses and arms
were swallowed up, but Edward wintered there in
his ships, which the Almighty had preserved.

About the middle of Lent, renewing his proposed
journey, Edward went up into his ship, and by Easter,
in fifteen days, came to Acre with a thousand chosen
men ; and he remained there for a whole month to
refresh his men and horses, and to learn the secrets of
the land. After the month, many of the Christians,
to the number of seven thousand, went forth with him
as far as twenty leagues from Acre, and they took
Nazareth, and killed all whom they found there. But,
returning to Acre, the enemy followed them close to
cut off all whom they could in narrow and enclosed
places; which when they saw, they turned back upon
them and drove them to flight, killing some of them.

About the feast of the Nativity of St. John the

Baptist, Edward, hearing that the Saracens were gathered together at Kakehowe, which was distant a short space from Acre, he went forth, and attacking them at daybreak, slew of them about a thousand men, the rest taking flight rapidly; and he carried away much spoil. Thence he went to the Pilgrims' Castle, which is situated on the sea, and remained there with the Christians that night, returning the next day to Acre.

In the meantime the King of Jerusalem sent to the great men of Cyprus that they should come with all speed; but they would not. But when Edward sent to them, praying them to come at his request, forthwith they came with many soldiers, saying that they owed him obedience, because his ancestors had formerly ruled their lands, and they ought always to be faithful to the kings of England. So the Christians being encouraged, they went forth three times from the feast of St. Peter ad Vincula to St. George, and having killed some, and finding no more to oppose them, they returned joyfully to their place again. Thus the fame of Edward grew great among the enemies of the Cross of Christ, and they feared him greatly, and took counsel together if haply they might destroy him secretly.

Then that great prince, the Emir of Joppa, sent letters to him feigning craftily that he wished to become a Christian, and that he could draw many to him, if they would be held in honour by him and the other Christians. And the thing pleased Edward, and he urged him to accomplish his purpose; and thus a second, and third, and fourth time he sent the same lad concerning this matter. But he was a messenger brought up by the Old Man of the Mountain, who neither dreaded death nor feared God. And when he came the fifth time, the servants of Edward having seen that he had neither knife nor arms in his hands or girdle, brought him into Edward's chamber; and he, bowing low, delivered to him letters from his lord, as he was wont to do. Now it was the Thursday in the octave of Pentecost, and about the hour of vespers, and on account of the heat Edward was sitting on his bed in his tunic only, with his head uncovered; and when the letters were read, it appeared that on the Saturday of the same week his lord would come to perform his promise. And the words pleased Edward, and they talked long concerning it. And the young man, bowing down before Edward, replied to his questions many times. Then putting his hand into his girdle, as if he would bring out secret letters, he drew out suddenly a poisoned knife, and struck at Edward as he lay. The prince, raising his hand to ward off the blow, was wounded deeply in the arm; but seeing him about to strike again, he threw him with such force that he fell to the ground, then seizing his hand he drew from it the knife, so violently that he wounded himself in the forehead, and plunged it into the assassin's side and killed him. And his servants, who had been at a distance, running up found him dead on the ground. One of them—it was his harper—seizing his stool, struck him on the head and knocked out his brains;

but Edward chid him for striking a dead man. And the evil tidings spread in the palace, and from the palace to the people, and they were much distressed. And the Master of the Templars, running to him in haste, gave him a precious draught to drink, lest the poison should spread in his body and harm him, saying reproachfully, 'Did I not warn thee of the treachery of this people? But,' he added, 'take comfort and fear not, for thou wilt not die from this poison.'

And his surgeons were called, and they dressed his wounds; but after a few days, seeing the flesh turning black, they began to speak one to another in low whispers; and there was no gladness among his servants.

Then he, perceiving this, said to them, 'Why talk you low? Can you not heal me? Fear not; but tell me.'

And one of them, an Englishman, answered, 'Thou canst be healed; but thou must suffer much.'

And he said, 'If I suffer, canst thou certainly promise me health?'

And he answered, 'I will promise it certainly, on pain of death.'

So he answered, 'I commit myself to thee; and do what thou wilt.'

And he said, 'Are there any of thy captains in whom thou trustest?'

And the Prince named several of those standing round; for there were many of his chief men standing round with his wife.

Then said the physician to the two whom he first named — Lord Edmund and Sir John de Vesci — 'Love you your lord?'

And they answered, 'Surely!'

And he said, 'Then take away his wife, and let not her lord see her until I give you leave.'

And they bore her away, weeping and lamenting; and they said, 'Suffer us, lady, for it is better that thou shouldest weep tears, than that all the land of England should weep.'

Then the surgeon cut away all the black flesh of his arm; and said, 'Take comfort, for I promise thee, that within fifteen days thou shalt go forth and mount thy horse.'

And what he had promised came to pass, and every one marvelled.

And when it was told to the great Sultan that Edward had survived, he would scarce give credit to it; and he sent to him three of his princes to excuse him, calling his gods to witness that it had not been done with his knowledge. And they fell flat on the ground before Edward, and worshipped him. But Edward said to them in English, 'You worship me, but love me not;' but they understood not his words, for they spoke with him by an interpreter. But he entertained them honourably, and after two days dismissed them in peace.

Then after a time there came mediators to bring about a truce; and they agreed to a truce for ten years, ten weeks, and ten days. So the Christians returned each one to his place. And the truce was made after Edward had been in Acre a year and a half. And about the Feast of the Assumption of the Blessed Virgin, he went up into his ship to return. And he came after seven weeks into Sicily to Trapani, and thence making his way by Palestrina, through Apulia, he came to Rome; where he was honourably received by Pope Gregory.

And when he came into France, and the fame of his glory spread among the people, many envied him, and chiefly the valiant Count of Chalons. So he sent to him, and prayed him that he would come and joust with him in his land. And he, not wishing to diminish his glory, though he might have excused himself because of his pilgrimage, yet would not, but willingly agreed; and it was proclaimed publicly that Edward, with his pilgrims, would hold a tournament against all comers. So they came together out of all those parts, on foot and on horse; and many conspired together to spoil the English, seiling beforehand their horses and arms, and drinking their Lebanon wine. And Edward also sent into England for certain of his great men; and there came to him earls and barons, till there were with Edward almost a thousand armed knights, and many foot-soldiers. But on the other side there were twice as many, both men and horses. And they coming together, the foot-soldiers began to spoil and rob; and our men resisted them with slings and bows and killed many, and drove the rest to the gates of the city; and many also fled to the water, and were drowned.

Then the Count, with fifty chosen knights, came

to Edward's troop and joined battle with him; and they fought together for a long space with swords, for they were both valiant men. And when the Count saw that he could not prevail with the sword, he threw his arms round the neck of Edward and enclosed him tightly. Then Edward said, 'Dost thou think to have my horse?' and he answered, 'I will have thee and thy horse too.' Then Edward, moved to anger, raised himself up and struck his horse so that it rushed forward, and the other, clinging round his neck, was dragged from his horse, and he flung him to the ground, so that for a long time he lay senseless; and Edward, astonished, gave him air to refresh him. And seeing their wickedness, and that they had already killed many of his men, and that they were fighting not as in a tournament but as in a battle, he said to his men, 'Let your eye spare no man, but do to them as they do to you.' So many met their deaths, and on all sides they raged with their swords. And the foot-soldiers returning from the slaughter of the others, when they saw many of their own men fallen, they entered boldly the battle of the horsemen, and stabbed the horses and cut the girths of many, so that their riders fell to the ground. Then Edward went to the Count, whom his men had lifted up and set on his horse, and he, being belaboured with blows, would have surrendered, but Edward at first would not accept it, but seeing his lack of courage, he bade him yield himself to a simple knight; and the rest fled, and many were left dead in that place.

When our men had thus obtained the victory and

Edward thought himself secure, it was told him that his men would be killed, as they entered the city, by the citizens. Then he sent for the mayor and chief citizens and bade them seize and punish the offenders, or else the next day he would set fire to the city and raze it to the ground. So they placed guards in all parts of the city and left Edward in peace. Thus much blood was shed at this meeting, whence the name of it was changed and it was called commonly, not the 'Tournament,' but the 'Little War of Chalons.'

Then Edward went to Paris and was honourably received by the King of the French. And after some days he went into Gascony, and remained there until he heard of the death of his father.

A GRANT OF LANDS FROM THE KING

CHAPTER VII.

THE SIEGE OF CAERLAVEROCK.

IN the year of grace one thousand three hundred, on St. John's Day, King Edward was at Carlisle, holding a great court, and he gave command that in short space all his men should array themselves and go with him against their enemies the Scots. Before the day set came, all the host that had been summoned was ready, and the King, with a great train, set out immediately against the Scots. They were mounted on horses of great value, and, to guard against surprise, well and heavily armed. There was unfurled many a banner and bright pennon set on a lance, and there was many a richly embroidered caparison of silk or satin. A long way off might be heard the neighing of the horses, and hills and valleys were covered with sumpter-horses and waggons bearing the victuals and the tents and pavilions. The days were fine and long, and the army marched by easy stages in four divisions. The first was led by the good Earl of Lincoln, and his banner was of saffron silk with a purple lion rampant. He was followed by many brave knights and barons, and with him rode the

Constable, the Earl of Hereford, a young man rich and personable. They led the van with caution, and rested not at night until they had searched well all dangerous passes. With them rode the marshals and the harbingers, to assign the places for lodging and encamping.

The second squadron was under the command of the Earl of Warren, who knew well how to lead noble and honourable men. His banner was of gold and azure chequered.

At a little distance came the third body, led by King Edward himself, king of England and Scotland, Lord of Ireland, Prince of Wales, and Duke of Aquitaine; and on his banner were three leopards of gold on red courant, proud and fierce, signifying how the King showed himself to his enemies, for his bite was not to be scorned, yet to those who sought his mercy and favour he was ever douce and debonair. His men were well ordered and arrayed, and by him rode his nephew, John of Brittany, who had left his father's house and served King Edward faithfully from his childhood. There rode many a baron and knight of noble birth and renowned for famous deeds, and their banners waving in the wind showed their name and degree.

Then followed the fourth squadron, with Prince Edward, the King's son, at its head. He was young in arms, for he was but seventeen years of age, but handsome in person, and well grown, and desirous to try his strength. He rode marvellously well, and he bore the arms of the King with a blue label. And

the King had given to him as guides and instructors
the noble Roger de Mortimer, and John de St. John,
and William le Latimer, who were well experienced
in war and very valiant men. With him rode also
his cousins, Thomas and Henry of Lancaster. There
also were the followers of the noble Bishop of Durham, the most valiant of the clergy of the kingdom,
and, in truth, of Christendom. He was a wise man
and could speak well, temperate and just, without
pride or covetousness. Yet he knew well how to
maintain his rights, and rode in the King's wars with
a noble following, well and costly arrayed. But, I
know not why, he could not himself ride to Scotland,
but sent of his men to help the King one hundred
and sixty men-at-arms. His banner he entrusted to
John de Hastings, whom he trusted and loved well.

The highroads to the castle of Caerlaverock were
all in the hands of the English, but it will not be
taken by check with a rook, for it was so strong that
it never feared a siege, and it was furnished with
men, engines, and victuals. In shape it was like a
shield, for it had only three sides in circuit, and in
each angle there was a tower. One was double, very
high, very long, and very wide; and below was the
gate, with a drawbridge, well made, and strong, and
well defended. There were good walls and good
ditches full of water, and I think I never saw any
castle more fairly situated, for on the west could be
seen the Irish Sea, and on the north a fair plain surrounded by an arm of the sea, so that no one can
approach it on two sides without danger from the

sea. On the south also the danger is not slight, for there are many places—woods, morasses, and ditches—into which the sea has entered, where it meets the river. It was necessary, therefore, for the army to reach it from the east, where the hills rise.

Then the King summoned his troops to take up their quarters in three companies. The valley was gay with gold and silver and every bright and pleasant colour. As soon as we were drawn up, and the marshals had allotted to us our places, there rose at once, without aid of carpenters or masons, houses of white or coloured cloth; the pins were driven into the ground, the cords were stretched. Many a great tree was felled to build huts, and leaves, grass, and flowers were gathered to strew inside. Thus our people took up their position, and those within the castle began to guess that they had never been in such peril before.

Then came our ships to land with the engines and victuals, and immediately the footmen marched to the attack. Stones, arrows, and quarrels began to fly, and those within did their work so well that in a little space many lay dead before the walls and others wounded and maimed.

When the men-at-arms saw the wounds of the foot-soldiers they rushed to the assault in furious haste. But the defenders threw stones on their heads, crushing helmets, and shields, and targets, and shouting with loud cries when they saw the evil they did them. There first was the good Bertram de Montbouchier and Gerard de Gondronville. The first was a Breton and the second a Lorrainer, and after him came Fitz-Marmaduke, with a choice following of brave men. There were Robert de Willoughby and Robert de Hamsart, Henry de Graham, and Thomas de Richmont, and they came on like men mad with rage and fury, and made their way up to the brink of the ditch. Then Richmont rushed on to the bridge, and demanded entrance, but they replied to him with great sharp stones. Willoughby, who followed him, received one in the breast, the worst of which his shield ought to have borne, but he disdained to use it. Fitz-Marmaduke stood firm as a rock, and Hamsart and Richmont drove back the stones with their shields as if they were at play.

Then came up to their aid a body of the King's followers, and also some of the Prince's men, with many a newly-painted shield and burnished helm. There I saw Ralph de Gorges, a new-dubbed knight, thrown to the ground by the force of the stones, but he would not deign to retire. Robert de Tony and Richard de Rokeley wrought much damage to the men on the walls, and made them oft retire; and Adam de la Ford undermined the wall as well as he could while the stones were flying as thick as rain. The Baron of Wigton and Kirkbride received many a heavy stone, but Kirkbride held before him his white shield with a green cross, and assailed the gate with blows like a smith with his hammer. Nevertheless, they were so bruised and weary with the blows of huge stones and the wounds of arrows and quarrels, that they were forced to retire.

But as soon as they were departed, Clifford, purposing that those within should have no repose, displayed his banner, and with him was Bartholomew de Badlesmere and John de Cromwell, who assailed the castle with stones till he was out of breath. Neither did the people of the chastelaine give them any rest; and little was left of the shield of Cromwell for him to carry from the field, so was it battered and crushed with the force of the stones.

After them came La Warde and John de Gray, and renewed the attack, but those within were waiting for them, and bent their bows and crossbows, and let fly upon them from their espringales. Then came up the men of my lord of Brittany, fierce as mountain-lions, and made a more furious assault than any who had gone before them, and my lord of Hastings' men, when John de Creting nearly lost his horse. Knight after knight came and showed his valour, and as one grew weary, another, fresh and stout, took his place.

But though the assault was so fierce and constant, those within made no offer of surrender, but defended themselves all that day, and all the night, and the next day, until tierce. Much mischief did them Brother Robert, who threw stones into the castle from a robinet unceasingly from dawn till night. He set up on the other side three still larger engines, and ceaselessly men bent them, loaded them with stones, and discharged them; and wherever they struck they shivered everything, nothing could resist their blows. Still the defenders yielded not, till one was wounded to death, and the roof was crushed in by the stones, and there was nothing to shelter them from the missiles.

Then they saw they could hold out no longer, and they hung out a flag, but he who held it was shot by an arrow through the hand into his face. So they cried out to cease, for they would yield to the King and come out to him. Then the marshals and the constable stopped the assault, and the defenders came out. And, behold, there were but sixty men, at which we marvelled greatly. And they were taken and brought under guard to the King, and he gave them their lives, and bade them give to each one a new gown.

So the castle was taken, and the King set up his banner, and the banners of St. Edmond, St. George, and St. Edward, and those of Segrave and Hereford, and the lord of Clifford, to whom the castle was given. And the King made his preparations, and went on his way through Galloway.

CHAPTER VIII.

THE BOLD DEEDS OF THE KNIGHTS OF SCOTLAND.

WHEN the young King, Edward III., had done justice on Sir Roger de Mortimer, and had shut up the Queen, his mother, in prison, he took new counsellors from among the wisest and best-trusted in all his land, and governed well and maintained his kingdom in peace through good counsel, and often held jousts, tournaments, and assemblies of ladies, and gained great favour in all his kingdom and great renown in all lands.

Thus he bore himself nobly while the truce lasted between him and the kingdom of Scotland. When the truce was at an end, and he was informed that the young King David had seized his city of Berwick, which belonged of right to his kingdom, and which the good King, Edward I., had always held quietly and in peace, and the young King's own father after him a long time, and that the kingdom of Scotland was held from him in fief, and that King David, his sister's husband, had not done him homage, he sent messengers to the young King David, and to his council, making request that he would desist from his good city of Berwick, for that it was his rightful heritage and had always belonged to his predecessors, the Kings of England, and that he would come to do homage for the kingdom of Scotland. And about this time it fell out that Messire Robert d'Artois, who was hated by the King of France, and had been driven out of France, and even out of Flanders and Brabant, came to England secretly, in disguise of a merchant, and came to the King and made himself known to him, for he was near akin to him, and he showed him how he was hated by the King of France, so that he could not find any land, lord, or country that would or dared support him, and, therefore, he was fled to him, who was of his lineage, and who would help him. And the noble King Edward was moved with great pity when he heard his complaints and his sufferings, and said that, though all the world should fail him, he would never fail him. And he made him of his council, and assigned him the county of Richmond for his maintenance, which had belonged to his predecessors, but the King held it from default of homage. And the King of Scotland having answered by his messengers that he would hold the town of Berwick, and would not yield it up, nor do homage for his kingdom, King Edward summoned a Parliament, and they gave him counsel that he should make preparation to enter the kingdom of Scotland, and regain the good city of Berwick. And when he heard their counsel he rejoiced greatly, and prayed them to meet him on a day assigned, each one arrayed according to his estate, at the New Castle upon Tyne. The day having come, the noble King Edward came to the New Castle, and waited for three days for the host to assemble. On the fourth day he departed, and went towards Scotland and towards Berwick. So he came into Scotland, and burnt and wasted all the plain country of Scotland, as far as Aberdeen, and took the largest towns, fortified with good ditches and palisades, and several castles, in which he put garrisons, for the young King David did not show himself in the plain. It is true that certain barons, lords, and other good men-at-arms, of which there were many in the country of Scotland, came often to skirmish with the army, and often there were great adventures and deeds of arms, with great prowess, on both sides, by which Walter de Manny acquired great fame and high favour with the King and all in the land, and was made knight by commandment of the King, being the one who most exposed himself. And the knights who came to skirmish with the English hid themselves in the wild country, and among marshes and great forests, where no one could follow them, but they followed the English so closely that almost every day there was fighting. And Sir Walter de Manny was always the most renowned, together with William de Montacute, who was a strong knight and brave, and he lost an eye at one of these jousts, and gained so great favour with the King that he made him Earl of Salisbury.

When this noble King Edward had thus wasted the plain country of Scotland at his pleasure, he returned to Berwick, which was well garrisoned and provided with valiant men-at-arms. Thus he could not win it as soon as he would, but tarried there a long time with all his host before he could get it, for those within maintained themselves well and loyally, so that there was many a deed of prowess done on one side and on the other. Those valiant men-at-arms also who held the forests and marshes made many great and bold assaults on the army by day and night, when they thought themselves most at peace, so that there were much loss and gain on one side and the other; and often these valiant men of Scotland went to fight those who were coming to the army, and the news of their deeds ceased not day nor night, and they captured the provisions that were being brought to the King. The greatest of them was the Earl of Moray, and, next after him, Sir William Douglas, the nephew of that valiant man who was killed in Granada as he was bearing the heart of King Robert of Scotland to the Holy Sepulchre. Of the rest I know not the names.

While King Edward lay before Berwick, the renown of him was carried into France, and many young knights and squires, who desired to bear arms and to adventure themselves, that they might come to honour, set out to go into those parts to serve the noble King of England, whose renown waxed greater from day to day. The young Count Jean de Namur, with Messire Guy and Messire Philippe, his two brothers, were thus desirous to go into those parts to see this young King of England and his state and that of the King of Scotland, and principally to see Messire Robert d'Artois, their uncle, for they knew that he was in the company of this King Edward. So they arrayed a fine company of men-at-arms, according to that which appertained to their degree, to make the journey. When they were ordered, furnished, and ready, they departed, and came to England, and asked the way to the place where the King was. And they showed them the way to London, and from London to York, and from York to Durham, and from Durham to the New Castle on the river of Tyne.

When they were come to the New Castle they rested themselves, and provided themselves with all that they might want in the host. While they tarried there, there came knights and squires from England, going to the host; at which these young lords were much rejoiced, and companied with them, that they might go more securely. There were also a great company of merchants, taking great provision to the host, and waiting for the company of men-of-arms. So it fell out, that the first night these young lords of Namur, and these knights and squires of England, and these merchants, lodged all together in an ancient town, which was called in the time of the Round Table of King Arthur, the Maidens' Castle. Very poorly were they lodged that night, and they passed it in great fear; for they found there none but poor women and little children who had nothing—for all the men of that country had lost all their goods, living in fear of the English, and the Scots also. So these lords, and their company, not being secure, that night they kept watch; and they sent out men to watch, that none might come to hurt them, and passed all the night in repairing and fortifying the walls, which were broken down and full of holes. But at break of day there came the young Earl of Moray, and Sir William Douglas, and many other knights and squires of Scotland, who, by their spies, knew well of the coming of these knights, and their doings. When those who were in the field heard the noise, they ran to the town, crying, 'To arms! to arms! the enemy is coming!' All came together at once, for they expected nothing else, and assembled where they could do most harm all together. When the day was come, they saw the Scots mounting the hill with a very great noise; and they defended themselves valiantly. But their defence would have availed them little, if the young Earl of Moray had not aided in saving the young lords of Namur; for the number of the Scots increased, and they assailed them behind and before, and on all sides; and they would have shown them no mercy, if they could have got them into their power. But when the Earl of Moray and Sir William Douglas saw the evil that would befall these young lords, they sprang to the front, and called upon them to render themselves up, for that if they waited till the foot-soldiers came upon them, they would not escape.

When these young lords heard that, and saw that their defence would not avail them, they listened to counsel, and yielded to these two lords; who took great pains to save their lives, and those of some of their companions. But few of the English could they save, for the footmen were already upon them and hewed them down; so that they were all killed, or but few escaped.

Thus these young lords could not achieve their enterprise, nor see the King, nor his host, nor their uncle; but were led prisoners into wild Scotland. And these lords of Scotland carried away all the provision that the English were conducting to the host before Berwick; which angered the gentle King Edward and all his host much, when they heard of the adventure, but they could not then amend it. I have never been able to know whether these lords of Namur were kept in prison, nor how long, nor if they were delivered; so I will leave them, and return to King Edward.

The noble King Edward dwelt a long time before the fair city of Berwick, for he would not leave it; and he assailed it many times. But there were within such good men-at-arms, that these assaults hurt them little, and they would never have rendered up the town if they had had enough victuals; but when victuals are lacking, one cannot hold out long, and it is better to bend than to break. This noble king would never leave the siege until he had his will; and he held the field so long, that the victuals failed in the town, and they could devise no way by which any could come to them from any part. So they endured much distress, and at last, when they could do no more, they yielded to the noble king after much parleying and treating, which would be too long to tell. And the King received them to mercy, their lives and goods being saved; and entered very nobly into the city with great feasting, and tarried there as long as he would. When he had dismissed his men, and sent back into their own country those whom he could spare; he put great garrisons and provisions in those castles which he had captured from the King of Scotland, in order to guard what he had conquered, placing still larger within and about the city of Berwick, for all were to yield obedience to it. And then he departed and returned into England, and held great feasts and courts, where the barons and lords of the country assembled, and gave great feasts, tournaments, jousts, and assemblies of ladies, by which he gained great favour with all; for all said he was a second King Arthur. And the men-at-arms and the garrisons which were left in Berwick, and the other strong towns, and castles, and fortresses, did well his commands, so that nothing was lost for a long time. But they had often to do with those lords who maintained themselves in the wild parts of Scotland and in the other castles, so that there were often skirmishes and pursuit.

Now you have heard how this gentle King of England conquered all Scotland, as far as the great forest which they call Jedburgh, where the savage Scots maintained themselves, because the forest is so perplexing and so full of great marshes, that none dare enter it unless he knows well the roads. And the young King David and his wife came into France to the King Philip with but few followers, for they were poor. And the King received them, and entertained them well. And Sir William Douglas—sister's son of

that other Sir William who died in Spain,—the young
Earl of Moray, Earl Patrick, Simon Fraser, and Alexander Ramsay, were still captains of the wild Scots,
and maintained themselves in these wild forests both
summer and winter for the space of seven years and
more, like very valiant warriors, and waged continual
war on the fortresses held by the King Edward,
meeting with many great adventures which it would
be too long to recount.

Now it happened that at the time that King
Edward was beyond the sea fighting in France, King
Philip sent men into Scotland, who came to the city
of St. John, and prayed these lords to bestir themselves and raise great war against the kingdom of
England; for that he would undertake that King
Edward should be away, and should leave them in
peace. Also he would aid them with men-at-arms
and money.

Therefore it happened that while Tournay was
being besieged, these lords of Scotland prepared, at
the request of King Philip, to make war on the
English. When they had assembled men enough,
they departed from the forest of Jedburgh and went
through Scotland — reconquering the fortresses as
many as they could—past the good city of Berwick
and across the river of Tyne, and entered the country
of Northumberland, which once was itself a kingdom.
There they found fat cattle in great numbers, and
wasted all the land and burnt it as far as the city of
Durham, and beyond; and then, turning to another
road, they went burning and wasting the land, so that

the King's country was greatly devastated by this inroad of four days. And then they returned into Scotland and reconquered their fortresses, except the city of Berwick and three other strong castles, of which one was called Roxburgh, another Stirling, and the third Edinburgh, which was the strongest, and was situated on a high rock which was seen in all the country round; and the ascent was so steep that a man could scarce climb it without resting two or three times, and a horse could only bear half a load. It was the castle which did most harm to the Scots, and the governor was a valiant knight named Sir Walter de Limosin. But this castle was taken daringly and with great subtilty, and all those in it put to death, as I will tell you.

When King Edward heard that these lords of Scotland were in his kingdom he was much enraged, and leaving France, he came quickly to London and took counsel what he should do. And he sent through all his kingdom and summoned his men to meet him at York at the end of a month, to go to destroy the remnant of the kingdom of Scotland. This was in the year of grace 1340, about All Saints' Day.

Now while they were assembling at York, the good knight, Sir William Douglas, bethought him of a great and perilous deed, and he discovered it to some of his companions,—to Earl Patrick, and to Simon Fraser (who had brought up the young King David), and to Alexander Ramsay, who all took part in this perilous deed. They took with them two hundred of the wild Scots to lay an ambush, as you shall hear. These four lords, who were all rulers of the Scots and knew each other's minds, went to sea with all their company, and with great provisions of oats, and white flour, and charcoal, and they came to a port about four leagues from this strong castle called Edinburgh, which hurt them more than the others. When they had arrived, they issued forth by night and took with them fifteen or eighteen of their companions whom they could best trust. And they put on poor, ragged coats, like poor merchants, and laded twelve little horses with twelve sacks of oats, flour, and charcoal, and left the rest in a ruined abbey at the foot of the mountain. When day broke, these merchants, who were armed beneath their poor garments, took the road and climbed the mountain; and when they were half way, Sir William Douglas and Simon Fraser went before, making the others follow gently. And they came to the porter and told him that with great fear they had brought corn, oats, flour and charcoal, and that if there was any wanted in the castle they would sell it cheap. The porter answered that they needed it much, but that it was so early that he could not awake the lords, but that if they would bring up their provisions he would open the first gate of the barriers. They heard this gladly, and made the others come, and entered the first gate. And Sir William Douglas saw that the porter had the keys of the great gate of the castle, and asked him which of them opened the little gate of it. Then they threw down their sacks in this first gate on the threshold, so that it could not be shut, and seized the porter and killed him so quietly that not a word was said, and took the keys. And they opened the gate of the castle, and Sir William blew his horn, and he and his companions threw off their poor clothes and threw down the sacks of charcoal in the gateway so that it could not be shut. When his other companions who were in ambush near the castle heard the horn, they climbed the mountain as fast as they could. The watch, who was asleep, heard the sound of the horn and awoke, and saw armed men climbing the hill, then he began to blow his horn and to cry, 'Treason! treason!' Then the Governor and the others awoke and armed themselves, and came to the gate and thought to shut it, but they could not, for William and his fifteen companions defended it. Then began a great fight between them, for those in the castle sought to save their lives, and the others to achieve their bold enterprise. And when those in the castle saw the ambush coming, they were much dismayed, and with all their power they sought to defend their castle; but at last, though they killed and wounded many, Sir William Douglas gained the castle and killed all within without mercy. And they tarried there that day, and ordained castellans and all the officers to keep the castle, and put a great garrison in it, and then returned joyful and glad to their companions in the forest of Jedburgh.

Thus this strong castle was taken by force and subtilty. When Sir William and his companions were returned to their men in the forest, there came to them the news that the noble King Edward was returned into England, and that he was assembling so many men that they could not stand against them. So they took counsel together what they should do, for they were but a few and badly arrayed, for they had warred long—for the space of seven years—and had rested and fed hardly, and they had no news of the King, their lord. So they were all wearied, and they agreed to send a bishop and an abbot to King Edward to pray for a truce. And the messengers found the King in the city of York, and he had with him six thousand men on horseback—knights and squires, and full sixty thousand on foot, to destroy all the remnant of Scotland. When the messengers saw that, they spoke and treated so that there was granted them a truce of a month on condition that they should send to King David of Scotland and require that within two months he should come to resist the power of England; and if he did not come, the said knights should give themselves up to King Edward. So the truce was granted, and messengers sent to France; and the Scots returned into Scotland.

CHAPTER IX.

SEA-FIGHTS.

Now the King of France held the lands of the King of England in Gascony, and the King Edward sent messengers to the King of France, praying him to yield them to him, for that they were his inheritance, and he had paid homage to the King of France for them. But he gave them a short answer. And about that time the Bishop of Glasgow came out of France with great provision of arms, horses, silver and gold, which the King of France had provided for the aid of the Scots in their war, and the worth of them was fifteen thousand pounds. But he was taken on the sea by Sir John Ros, and carried into the port of Sandwich, and soon after the bishop died of grief. And not long after the Normans entered into Portsmouth in great strength, and set on fire the whole town, and killed many of the English, and took whatever they could find, and then without delay went away. For they entered under the arms of England, and so deceived the people of the town; but, yet, certain English came upon them and killed many of them in the retreat.

And the next year, when the King of France heard how alliance had been made between the Emperor and King Edward, he assembled a great number of men, and gathered together no small fleet to attack the lands of England with great daring, and they did what evil they could without pity by land and sea. And they landed at Southampton, and killed all they could find, and lay hands on everything, hanging some of the noblest of the town in their own houses, and gave the whole town to the flames; but some of the people coming to the help of the town, they went on board of their ships and escaped to the high sea. But that year Edward, duke of Cornwall, the son of the King, held a parliament in London, whereat was ordained that they should keep guard in five ports with sixty ships full of armed men. The Earl of Huntingdon, Constable of England, was made Warden of Suffolk, and Lord Robert de Morley Warden of Norfolk. And that year the winter was severe and beyond measure long. Then, about Easter came the Normans with twelve galleys and eight spynaces, with about four thousand men, and they came to Southampton; and when they saw the boldness of the English, prepared and ready for defence, they did not dare to set foot on English land, but went out to sea lest the English should follow them. But the English offered to let them come on shore to refresh themselves for two days, if they would agree after the two days to fight together, ten against ten, or twenty against twenty, or in any other way that they might agree to.

But they would not, but went away without doing anything.

Then, in the year 1339, about the feast of the Trinity, there came enemies to the port of Hastings and burnt a great part of the town, and on St. James' day came the French in great strength to the port of Sandwich, and they had thirty-two galleys, and twenty large ships, and fifteen smaller ones, but they did not dare to land on account of the English being prepared, but turned away to the port of Rye, and did much evil there. But the English came upon them on the sea, and the French took to flight, and the English pursued them to Boulogne de Notre Dame, and set on fire a great part of the town, and hanged twelve of the ships' captains, and returned to England with the captured ships. About the same time Robert de Morley, the Admiral, sailed to Normandy with his ships, and with the ships of the Cinque-ports, and they burnt many towns, Ryes and other ports: and also burnt the fleet of the Normans, about eighty ships. After that all the galleys from the coasts of France, with the rest of the ships, assembled at Sluys, in Flanders, and before the Flemings there they took an oath, with a solemn vow, that they would not return home until they had taken a hundred ships of the English, and set on fire five hundred towns in England; but by the disposal of God their vain imaginings came to nought. For the Saturday after the feast of St. Michael they took their way on the high seas, and a tempest coming upon them, they fell into extreme peril, and many of their ships being lost, and the greater part of the men drowned, the rest returned to the land of Flanders.

After this the King of France considered within himself how he might hinder and impede the King Edward, and prevent him returning, as he proposed, into the land of Flanders. So he assembled a very large and noble fleet of ships, such as cannot be seen in these degenerate days, and filled them with armed men and cross-bowmen, and they came to Flanders to the port of Sluys, that they might take King Edward coming to his queen, then dwelling in Ghent. Then King Philip of France sent to the Pope, and certified him that King Edward would not cross the sea, but that either he would be killed or captured. And he stirred up the Scots to rise and make war in England, and sent into Flanders about thirty thousand armed men, and forty thousand foot-soldiers, nobly arrayed, to destroy the islands of Flanders, because the nobles of Flanders had sworn faith to King Edward. But the Flemings sent to the King of England that he should come to them quickly with aid, or it would be necessary for them to yield to King Philip, and the Count of Flanders and Queen Philippa with her children would be taken.

Then King Edward, understanding the purpose of the King of France, made his fleet assemble with all speed to carry him over into Flanders, and put to sea, having with him Henry de Burghersh, bishop of Lincoln, a man of nobility, wise in counsel, of rare boldness, and great strength, and well known for his retinue of strong men. And there came also

SEA FIGHT

Henry, the noble young Earl of Derby, afterwards the first Duke of Lancaster, and the Earl of Northampton, the Earl of Gloucester, the Earl of Huntingdon, and many of the great men of the kingdom. And thus, on the vigil of St. John the Baptist, about the third hour, that is, on Friday, King Edward and his ships came to the coasts of Flanders near Blanckenburg, and there they saw all the ships of the navy of France lying in the port of Sluys. Then King Edward sent Lord Reginald de Cobham, Sir John de Cundy, and Sir Stephen de Laburkin, to explore and reconnoitre the fleet in its array; and they, riding along the land, came so near to it that they could see well the apparelling of it, and they saw about nineteen ships greater and more excellent than they had ever seen before; one of which, for its excellence, was named the *Christopher*. And they saw besides two hundred ships of war in the water near the land, arrayed in three lines, with other smaller boats and barges. The next day, that is to say, St. John the Baptist's day, the fleet came out of the port of Sluys at Grongue, disposed in order as has been described. And King Edward, seizing the favourable opportunity, that same day, at the ninth hour, sailed with his ships towards them through the deep sea, not fearing either their ferocity nor the superiority of their numbers. And the battle began and was fought bravely and fiercely; but the Lord gave the victory to King Edward, so that the French were overthrown, and they fled in great ships called *St. Denis* and *St. George*, with Sir Hugh

Quiriel, who was their chief captain, and Nicholas Bychet, who the same day was made knight and killed with Sir Hugh. And it is said that there fell of the French and their allies, our enemies, about twenty-five thousand men. And in the middle of the night following twenty-three ships and barges of the Norman fleet escaped from us and were not taken. But King Edward landed in Flanders, and with the Flemings and his whole army went to the town of Tournay and laid great siege to it.

CHAPTER X.

THE BLACK PRINCE AT POITIERS.

Now there came from the country of Gascony the valiant and preux Captal de Buch, and he, being great in renown and much loved by all, was received with great joy and much feasting; and he told the King that many valiant knights in Gascony were faithful to his cause, and had fought with much toil and pain for his honour, only they had no chief of his blood to lead them, but that if the King would send one of his sons they would be much emboldened. Then the King assembled his parliament, and all agreed to send the Prince into Gascony, for that he was held in so much honour. And with him should go the noble Earl of Warwick, and the Earl of Salisbury, and Ufford, earl of Suffolk, and the Earls of Oxford and Stafford, and bold Sir Bertram de Burghersh, Sir John de Montague, and Lord Le Despenser, Sir Walter Manny, the good Reginald de Cobham, who had been present at many an assault, and there, too, were Chandos and Audley. And they were all ordered to assemble at Plymouth in their ships men-at-arms, and archers, and a great store of victuals;

and in two months the Prince took leave of the King his father, and the Queen his mother, and his brothers and sisters, and, amidst much weeping and lamentation, bade them adieu and went on his way. And he rode night and day till he came to Plymouth, and bade them carry on board the ships the victuals and the armour, hauberks, helmets, lances, shields, bows and arrows; and the horses also were put on board. Then he, with all his noble knights, the very flower of chivalry, put to sea and sailed till they came to Bordeaux. The noble barons of that country, little and great, came out to meet him—the Prince d'Albret, the Lord of Montferrat, and, in truth, all the barons of Gascony. And the Prince stayed in Bordeaux until all his array were disembarked and his horses refreshed. Then he took the field with more than six thousand fighting-men, and rode towards Toulouse, taking Carcassonne, Beziers, and Narbonne, subduing all before him, and wasting the land, and in winter returned in triumph to Bordeaux, and his troops took up their quarters in the castle. The Earl of Warwick lodged at La Role, and Salisbury near by at St. Foy, and Suffolk with his men at St. Emillion. Chandos and Audley, with the loyal Captal, lodged in the fields, and had oft to fight to hold their ground. And they held the land between Cahors and Agen, and took the Port Ste. Marie, and thus, riding up the river, attacked Perigueux, and lodged there a great part of the winter.

When the summer was come the Prince assembled his forces and marched upon Saintonge, and he took the tower of Romorantin by assault, and took prisoner the Sire de Boucicault and the Lord de Craon, and many others. More than two hundred were taken, men of renown; and he rode on through the land as far as Tours.

Then King John was greatly moved, and assembled all his forces, and no duke nor baron stayed behind. There came to the meeting-place of Chartres more than ten thousand men, and without delay they set forward towards Tours. And when the Prince heard of them he took the road towards Poitiers. On Saturday they were attacked by the Count de Joigny and the Count d'Antoire; but the Frenchmen were all taken or slain. King John and the Prince marched to meet each other, and pitched their tents so near one another that they watered their horses in the same river.

Then there came the Cardinal Perigord and prayed the King's leave to ride to the Prince and see if he would not make peace, that the blood of so many men might not be shed. And the King answered, 'Cardinal, we are very willing you should ride to the Prince; but understand well, we will agree to nothing but that he gives up all the castles and land that he has seized since he came from England, and consents to abandon the quarrel altogether.'

So the Cardinal rode to the Prince's army, and implored him to have pity on the lives of men and listen to the terms of peace. And the Prince answered that his quarrel was just and good, and that his father, King Edward, was the rightful heir of France, of which Philip of Valois had been crowned king; but that he would not hinder the making of peace if it could be effected. 'But,' said he, 'I can do nothing in this matter without the King, my father, further than to agree to a truce and arrange for treating of peace.'

And the Cardinal returned to the King, and the King assembled the barons of both sides, and laid the matter before them. And there was the Count of Tancarville, archbishop of Sens, De Thalrus, Chargny, Boucicault, and Clermont; and on the English side the Earls of Warwick and Suffolk, Sir Bertram de Burghersh, Audley, and Chandos. What was counselled I know not, but they could not be accorded. And when they were about to depart one from the other, Sir Geoffroy de Chargny said, 'Since we cannot make peace, let a hundred be chosen from each side, and let them fight together. And the hundred that is discomfited let all that army be counted discomfited, and leave the quarrel and depart from the field. It will be better thus than that so many be killed.' And to that the Earl of Warwick replied, 'Sir, what would you gain by that? You know well that you have four times as many men-at-arms as we have, and we are on your land. Here is the field, and a fit place. Let every one do his best, for I will agree to no other way; and may God uphold the right!'

So they returned each man to his army, and on both sides it was said that the Cardinal had betrayed them; but he departed grieving, and rode to Poitiers.

Then the King of France put his army in array,

fearing that the Prince would escape him. And he called the Marshal de Clermont, and d'Audenham, and the noble chieftain, the Duke of Athens, and gave them the command of the vanguard, with three thousand men and two thousand servants, with swords and lances and two thousand arbalesters, and bade them show no mercy to the English. Then he called his son, the Duke of Normandy, and said to him, 'Fair son, you will be King of France after me, therefore lead the second division, and the Duke of Bourbon you shall have as companion, and the Lord of St. Venant and the good Tristan de Magnelers will carry your banner. Cry, "For John!" and spare no Englishman, small nor great. Put them all to death, that none of them may ever dare to cross the sea again.'

So the army of the Dauphin was put in array, with banners and pennons resplendent with purple, gules and ermine unfurled to the wind, and the trumpets and drums sounded till the earth rang again. And it took up its place on one side; four thousand of them there were, and many a good knight among them.

The rear-guard he gave to the Duke of Orleans, his brother, with three thousand fighting-men, and bade him 'show no mercy to the English, but put them all to death, for they have done us much harm and burnt and destroyed our land.'

And when the noble King John had arrayed his forces he went to the fourth division, and three of his sons were with him, and the Dukes of Anjou and

Berry, and Philippe le Hardi, who was very young, and Jacques de Bourbon, and many more than I can name, for there were twenty-three banners. And there were four thousand armed horses, all knights of the best escutcheons, led by Guichard d'Angle, and the Lord d'Aubigny, and Eustace de Ribaumont.

And on the other side the Prince put his men in array, but if he could he would have avoided a battle. Then he called the Earl of Warwick to him and said, 'Sir, since we must fight, I pray you take the vanguard, and with you shall be the noble Lord de Pomiers, and all his brothers, who are valiant and bold. Pass the road and protect our baggage. I will ride after you with all my knights, and support you, and the Earl of Salisbury will follow you with the rear-guard.' So they passed the night with little rest, for there was constant skirmishing. When morning came the brave Prince sent for Sir Eustace d'Abrichecourt and the Lord of Courton, who was as brave as a lion, and bade them go reconnoitre the French army. Then each mounted his horse, but they rode too near, and were both of them taken, at which the Prince was much grieved.

Then a great noise arose, and the Prince left his quarters and mounted his horse; but he hoped still to avoid a battle. But the French cried aloud to their King that the English fled, and that they would escape. And they mounted and began to advance; and the Maréchal d'Audenham cried, 'We shall lose them all if we do not fall upon them at once;' but the Maréchal de Clermont answered, 'Nay, brother, you make too much haste,—the English flee not; rather will they soon be here.' 'If you linger thus,' said d'Audenham, 'we shall lose them all.' Then Clermont answered in anger, 'Maréchal, you are too bold; but by Saint Denis, I will be so far in front of you this day that the point of your lance shall not reach my horse's saddle!' Thus in anger they rode on, and the battle was joined, and each side began to assail the other. The Prince had given the rearguard to the Earl of Salisbury, but he was that day the first engaged, for the marshals came down upon him in fury; and when he saw the battle turning his way, he cried aloud, ' Advance, sirs; since we who were the last are now become the first; let us do as shall win us honour.' And they approved themselves well; but it was a marvellously hard fight, and many a man met his end. The archers drew their arrows to the head, and never did arrows fly more straight. They were posted on each side of the road by the side of the men-at-arms. Then came pricking the preux chevalier, Sir Guichard d'Angle, right into the mêlée, and the Maréchal Clermont, and Eustace de Ribaumont, and the Lord d'Aubigny; but the Earl of Salisbury and his companions, brave as lions, discomfited the marshals and their armed knights before the vanguard could turn to help them, for they were on the other side of the road. And there they joined, and in one company fell upon the Dauphin; and so fierce was the attack that the French, dismayed, began to give ground and to turn their backs and

N

mount their horses. Then rose a shout of 'Guienne Saint George!' and the Dauphin turned and fled, and his men gave way, and many were killed and taken.

But while the English were pursuing, the King of France advanced upon them with a great force, but the Prince, putting his trust in Heaven, cried, 'Advance, banners! and let every man think of his honour!' and by his side were the two brave knights, Chandos and Audley. And as the fight began, Audley prayed the Prince humbly, and said, 'Sir, I have made a vow that when I shall see the banner of the King of France, I will be the first to charge. I pray you give me leave, for it is high time.' And the Prince answered, 'James, have your will.' And Sir James, without delay, rode forward a spear's length before the others and fell fiercely on the enemy. But the others were not slow to follow with lowered lances, and bravely fought Chandos, Warwick, and Le Despenser, Montagu, Sir Ralph de Cobham, good Bertram de Burghersh; and in another part, Lord Salisbury and Lord Oxford, and the Gascon captain Captal. Many a marvellous blow was given and many a man fell, and the fight lasted long; but again and again sounded the voice of the Prince, 'Advance, sirs! win this place as we value life and honour!' And at last the victory turned to him, and his enemies gave way and fled; and King John, fighting bravely with his knights round him, was taken, and Philip his son, and many a high banneret whose name I cannot tell, but there were a good sixty of them; and of others, more than a thousand. Of those who died, were the Duke of Bourbon, and the noble Duke of Athens, the Maréchal Clermont, and many others; more than three thousand lay dead. And the English rejoiced, shouting 'Guienne Saint George!' And this battle was fought in the year one thousand three hundred and fifty-six, on the nineteenth day of September.

Then to the noble Prince, preux chevalier in word and deed, was brought King John; and the Prince entertained him well, and to honour him more, himself aided him to disarm. That night the Prince lodged on the field, in a little pavilion among the dead, with his men round him; but little anyone slept. And the next morning they set out on the road to Bordeaux with their prisoners. And when they reached Bordeaux, all the people came out to meet them with processions and crosses, chanting orisons, and the women and girls, young and old: there was marvellous great joy. There the Prince remained all the winter; and he sent a messenger to the King, his father, and the Queen, his mother, with news of his doings, and prayed that vessels might be sent in which the King of France might be conveyed to England.

When the news reached the King, he rejoiced greatly, and, joining his hands, thanked God; and the Queen also thanked God that she had a son so brave: and the vessels were sent to Bourdeaux. The Prince made no long delay, but put on board all his array, and the King and the other prisoners, and sailed to England. When the King heard that they had landed, he summoned his barons to go and meet them, and went himself with more than twenty earls and conveyed the Prince to London. Never was such joy seen before. There was the great King, and the Queen his wife, and his mother, and many a lady and fair damsel; and there was dancing, and feasting, and jousting, as in the days of King Arthur.

And King Edward collected a large army and crossed over to France, and rode through Artois, Picardy, Champagne, and Burgundy, and came before Paris and drew up in battle array, but they fought not, for peace was made and the two kingdoms were accorded. King John was delivered from prison and Guienne given up to the noble Prince. And this peace was made in the year one thousand three hundred and sixty, in the sweet month of May, when the nightingale sings and birds are no longer sad. And the two kings met at Calais, with the Prince and all the chivalry of England and France, and there they swore on the Book and on the Holy Sacrament that they would keep the peace without falsehood and without any renewing of the war. So the King of France returned to his kingdom, and the noble King Edward and the Prince, with great joy to England.

How peace was proclaimed between the kingdoms of France and England.

CHAPTER XI.

THE JOUSTS OF SAINT INGHELBERTH.

Of the Enterprise of the three Knights.

THERE were three valiant knights of France, to wit, Sir Boucicault the Younger, Sir Regnault de Roye, and the Lord de Saint-Py, who undertook to be under arms during the summer, on the frontier of Calais, to meet all comers, knights or esquires, being foreigners, during the term of thirty days, and to joust with whomsoever would, with blunted lances or otherwise.

Now since the enterprise of the three knights seemed to the King of France and to everyone somewhat presumptuous, he showed them how it would be for the best to write the terms of it on a sheet of paper that the King and his council might see and consider it; and if anything out of order should appear in it, they would cancel or amend it, for the King and his council would allow nothing to be done that was unreasonable.

To this demand the three knights answered and said, 'What you say is right, and we will do it willingly.' So they took a clerk, and ink, and paper, and shut themselves into a room, and the clerk wrote the terms of their challenge :—

'For the great desire that we have to see and to have the acquaintance of noble gentlemen, knights and esquires, strangers, of the kingdom of France, and of other more distant kingdoms, we intend to be at Saint Inghelberth, the twentieth day of May coming, and to be there thirty days together; and each day excepting the Fridays, we will be ready to ride five courses with any knight or esquire, being gentlemen and strangers, from whatever country, who choose to come, with a sharp or blunt lance, as he pleases, or with both. Our shields will be to be found on the outside of our tents, painted with our arms,—that is to say, our shields of war and our shields of peace.

'And whoever will joust, let him come or send the day before to touch with a wand whichever he may choose ; and if he touch the shield of war, the next day he shall have the joust of war; and if he touch the shield of peace, he shall have the joust of peace. And it is agreed that whoever will touch or send to touch, shall tell or shall have told their names to the persons to whom we shall commit the care of our shields. And all the foreign knights or esquires who wish to joust shall bring with them each a noble friend, and we will do the same on our part, and these shall take order for everything that is to be done.

'And we pray all noble knights and esquires who may come, that they will not think or imagine that we do this thing from pride, hatred, or ill-will, but only in order to see them, and to have their noble company and acquaintance, which is what we desire with all our hearts.

'And none of our shields shall be covered with steel or iron, any more than those belonging to those with whom we shall joust; and no other advantage, fraud, or deceit, shall be used, except such as may be allowed by those to whom the care of the jousts is committed by both parties.

'And that all noble gentlemen, knights and esquires, who may take knowledge of this thing, may hold it as true and authentic, we have sealed these letters with the seals bearing our arms.

'Given at Montpellier, the twentieth day of November, in the year of grace, thirteen hundred and eighty-nine.'

And underneath was written:—

'Regnault de Roye,
'Boucicault,
'Saint-Py.'

The King of France was greatly pleased with this high and courageous enterprise of the three knights. But before he would consent that the thing should take place, the work was very well examined and considered, lest any wrong should be understood by it. And it seemed to some that were called to the council that the thing was not reasonable, in that the place was so near to Calais, and that the English might take it for arrogance and presumption; which it was needful to consider well, for a truce for three years had been made and sworn to between France and England, so that nothing was to be allowed which might bring about dissension between the two kingdoms. The council were more than a day in considering this matter, and they knew not what to do, and would have broken it off, for those who were wise said that it was not good to consent to all the proposals of the young knights, and that as much evil as good might come of it. Nevertheless the King, who was young, inclined to the side of his knights, and said, 'Let them do their emprise; they are young and of high courage, and have sworn and vowed before the ladies of Montpellier; it is our will that the thing begin and be carried out according to their loyal power.'

When they saw the King's inclination no one ventured to contradict or withstand him, at which all the knights rejoiced, and it was agreed that it should take place according to the form and manner written and sealed by the three knights. The King sent for these to his chamber, and said to them, 'Boucicault, Regnault, and you, Saint-Py, see that you defend the honour of yourselves and of the kingdom well in this matter, and spare nothing in maintaining your rank and state, for we will be answerable for you up to ten thousand francs.' Then the three knelt before the King, and returned him many thanks.

Then the three knights took great pains to accomplish their desire and fulfil their promise; for they notified and published it everywhere, especially in the kingdom of England, where it was heard gladly, and by it many knights and esquires were pricked to the heart. The younger of them, who longed to distinguish themselves, pondered much what they should do in the matter. Some among them said that great blame and reproach would be theirs if, the place being so near Calais, they did not cross the sea and see and fight with these knights. I will name those who chiefly held this language. First, Sir John Holland, earl of Huntingdon, the brother of the King of

England, and Sir Peter Courtenay, besides Sir John Drayton, Sir John Walworth, Sir John Russel, and many other, more than a hundred in all, who said, 'Let us arrange to go across to Calais, for these knights of France have ordered this game only that they may see and know us. Certainly they have done well and they are good companions. Let us not fail them.'

The thing was made so public in England that those who had no desire themselves to fight declared they would be there on the appointed day to look on. So these and those who would fight sent over their arms and their horses and equipage before them; then when the day itself drew near they crossed the sea. Sir John Holland was the first to go, and more than sixty knights and squires with him, and he came to Calais and lodged there.

At the beginning of the fair month of May the three young knights of France were prepared and ready. They came first to Boulogne-sur-Mer, and tarried there some days, and then departed and came to the Abbey of St. Inghelberth. Being there, they heard what plenty of knights and squires had come out of England and were now at Calais. At this they rejoiced much, and to hurry on the work and in order to warn the English, they sent to have three vermilion-coloured pavilions, very fine and rich, pitched on the plain between St. Inghelberth and Calais; and at the entrance of each pavilion in front were hung two shields bearing the arms of the knights—the shield of peace and the shield of war.

Of the First Day.

Now, on the 21st day of May, as had been proclaimed, the three knights were ready, with their horses, ordered and saddled as the joust required; and the knights and squires, desirous of tilting or of seeing the combat, came out of Calais and rode to the place, where they drew up on one side. The place of the tournament was large and wide and smooth, and well grassed. Sir John Holland was the first to begin, and he sent a squire to touch the war-shield of Sir Boucicault. Then Sir Boucicault came out of his pavilion, ready armed, and mounted his horse, and took his shield and a good lance, strong and well made; then the two took up their distances, and when they had well eyed one another, they spurred and came, without sparing themselves, with great force against one another, and the spear of Sir Boucicault pierced the Earl of Huntingdon's shield, and the point ran along his arm, but without wounding him. Then the knights passed on and stopped in their positions. This course was much praised. In the second they struck one another slightly, but did each other no harm; and in the third the horses refused the course.

The Earl of Huntingdon, who was heated and would fain go on with the joust, came back to his place, expecting that Sir Boucicault would take up his lance. But this he did not do, and signified that he would do nothing more that day with the Earl.

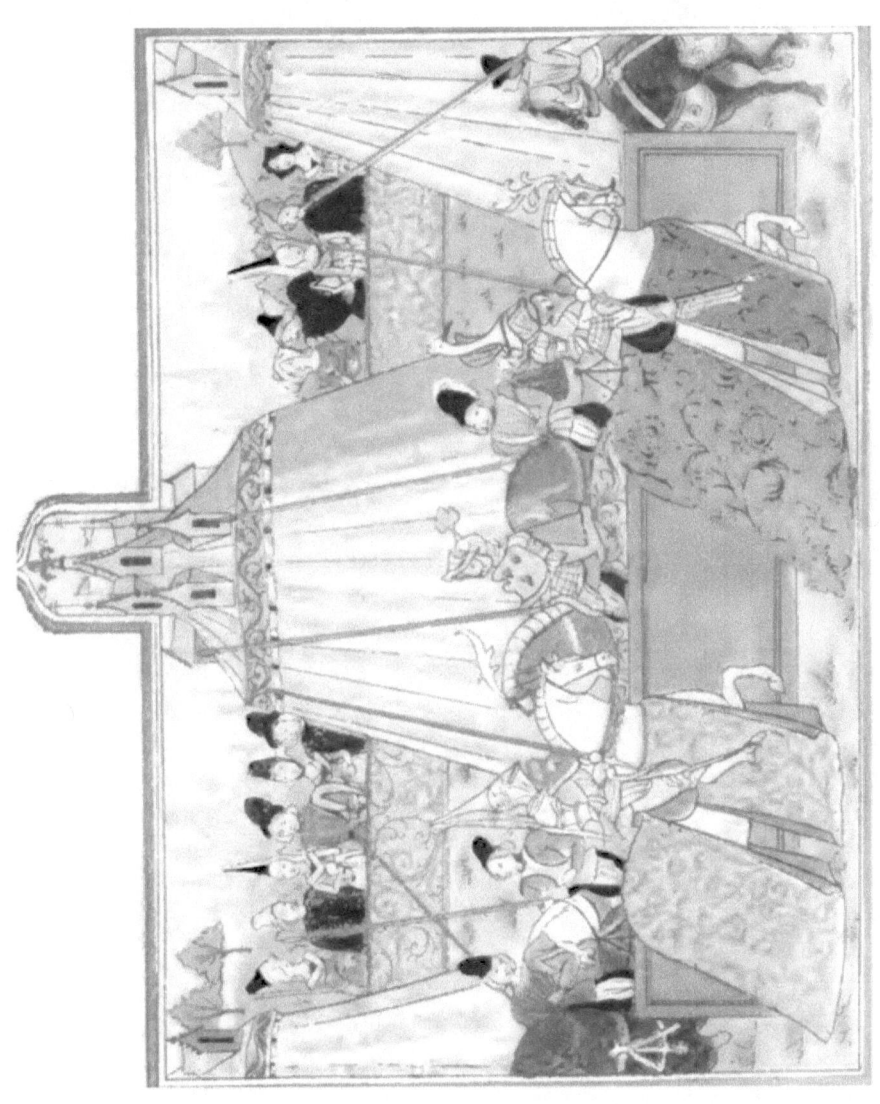

When the Earl saw that, he sent his squire to touch the war-shield of the Lord de Saint-Py, and he, who never refused, came from his tent, and mounted and took his shield and lance; and when the Earl saw that he was ready for the tilt, he spurred his horse with right good will, as did Saint-Py, couching their lances. But as they met the horses crossed, and in this crossing the Earl was unhelmed.

So he returned to his men and put on his helmet, and grasping his lance and the Lord de Saint-Py his, they met full, striking their shields with great force, so that they would both have been unhorsed if they had not kept their saddles by clasping the horses firmly with their legs; so they returned to their places and refreshed themselves a little, taking breath and cooling themselves. Sir John Holland, who had a great love of arms, took his lance again; and when the Lord de Saint-Py saw him coming, he did not refuse, but met him as well as he could. The two knights encountered one another so that the lances rang on the steel helmets, and the red sparks flew, and the Lord de Saint-Py was unhelmed.

This course was greatly praised, and both French and English said that the three knights had tilted well, neither sparing nor doing themselves damage. The Earl of Huntingdon desired to run yet another course for the love of his lady, but it was refused him. So Sir John left the lists to make room for another, for he had run his courses well, and gained much honour from all sides.

Then advanced a gentle English knight, who was

called the Earl Marshal, and he sent to touch the war-shield of Sir Regnault de Roye; and this being done, Sir Regnault came out of his pavilion, fully armed, and mounted his horse, which was standing ready. They hung his shield round his neck and buckled it, and he took his lance. The knights spurred their horses with great violence, but they failed in the first course because the horses swerved, at which they were greatly enraged. In the second Sir Regnault was struck and his own lance was broken. In the third they struck each other on the helmets with such force that fire flew from them, and the Earl Marshal was unhelmed. He returned to his place and did no more that day, for he had done enough. Then came forward Sir Thomas Lord Clifford, a valiant knight and cousin to Sir John Chandos, who was so famous and brave a knight; he sent to touch the war-shield of Sir Boucicault. The two knights came on with prodigious force, and struck each other on the helmets till the sparks flew, but the lances did not break nor the knights lose their stirrups, but passed on and stopped to take their places for the second course with great good-will. They spurred their horses and met without sparing one another. Sir Boucicault broke his lance and was unhelmed, but did not lose his seat. Sir Thomas Clifford prepared to tilt again with Boucicault, but Boucicault did not put on his helmet.

Then Sir Thomas resolved to tilt with another, and sent to touch the shield of the Lord de Saint-Py, who came at once out of his tent and mounted and took shield and lance, and prepared to joust. They met with great force, and Sir Thomas broke his lance into three splinters on the shield of Saint-Py, who struck him on the helmet and unhelmed him, and then passed on. The Lord Clifford returned to his people and did nothing more that day, for they said he had borne himself well and honourably.

After this a gentle knight of England, named Sir Henry de Beaumont, sent to touch the shield of Sir Boucicault, who was ready to answer, having just tilted with Sir Thomas, Lord Clifford: The two spurred with great force; but Sir Henry did not use his lance well, and struck Sir Boucicault sideways, while Boucicault struck full in the middle of his shield and bore him to the ground, and passed on. The knight rose, and was helped by his people to remount. Then the Lord de Saint-Py came forward, and they tilted two courses very courteously, without any damage to either.

Sir Peter Courtenay, who had a great desire to run six courses, sent to touch all the three shields of war, which caused great astonishment; and he was asked what he meant by it. He answered, that it was his pleasure to run two courses with each of the three French knights, if no mischief should happen to him meanwhile; and he prayed them to grant him them, which they did.

Sir Regnault de Roye came forward the first; but this first course failed, for the horses refused it, which filled them with rage. So they returned to their places, and spurred again carrying their lances straight, so that this second course did not fail. Sir Regnault unhelmed the English knight, and his two courses being run he returned to his place. Sir Peter Courtenay being re-armed, met the Lord de Saint-Py full gallop, each breaking his lance against his adversary's helmet. They received fresh ones, and in the second course the Lord de Saint-Py struck Sir Peter sideways, owing to his horse swerving a little. Sir Peter unhelmed him, and then passed slowly on to his place.

Then Sir Boucicault came forward, and Sir Peter met him. They met with such a rude shock that the horses stood stock-still in mid-career; but no damage followed. They unhelmed one another in the second course. The six courses being thus run, Sir Peter asked as a favour that he might run one more with any of the three knights who might choose; but this was refused, and he was told that he had done enough for that day.

Another English knight came forward named Sir John Walworth, fully armed, and sent his squire to touch the war-shield of Sir Regnault de Roye. The knight was ready to reply to the summons, and both advanced full gallop, hitting each other on the helmet very sore; yet neither was unhelmed, nor were the lances broken. The second course was spoilt through the swerving of the horses, which greatly vexed them. The third lance they broke in the very centre of their shields. The fourth course was run without anything being done; but the fifth was only too well employed, for they unhelmed one another, and then each returned to his own party.

Sir John Russel, a very expert and valiant English knight, well known in divers countries, was the next. He sent to touch the Lord de Saint-Py's shield, who was already armed and on horseback. They met with such force with the lances against each other's shield that the horses were stopped short in mid-career. They were not long in returning to their places and beginning the second course, which was spoilt however, for just as they should have met, the horses swerved and refused the encounter, so that they failed of their stroke. In the third course they struck each other with such force on the visors that both were unhelmed. The English knight returned to his men and tilted no more that day.

Thereupon, a young English knight of very high courage, named Sir Peter Sherburn, sent to touch the war-shield of Sir Boucicault. The knight was ready and mounted, leaning on his spear and waiting for an adventure. So when he saw that he was challenged to joust, he couched his lance and looked to see what his adversary would do, and seeing that he was handling his horse, he began to rouse his own. Then spurring and couching their lances, they hoped to meet fair, but were disappointed by the swerving of their horses. They returned to their places determined to manage them better; and the next course was so well performed that they hit each full in the visor. Sir Boucicault broke his lance, and the English knight used his with such force that he unhelmed Sir

Boucicault so violently that the blood gushed from his nose. Then Sir Boucicault returned to his pavilion, for it was near upon vespers. But Sir Peter Sherburn would not cease till he had completed his courses; so he sent to touch the war-shield of Saint-Py, who was ready to answer. They spurred their horses as straight towards each other as they could and struck one another on the helmets; but the lances slipped and they passed on without hurt. Those who were watching said that if the lances had been pointed lower, so that they had struck on the shields, one or both must have been borne to the earth. In the next course they met, striking each other so full upon the shields that both lances flew into three pieces, and the Lord de Saint-Py made the Englishman lose his stirrups and fall on the earth. He rose at once and was aided by his people to retire to his side. The Lord de Saint-Py returned to his place, viewing the English array, and showing that he was ready to tilt again, either with the knight whom he had just overthrown, or with any other; but none came forward, for it was time to cease for the day and to retire to their inns.

The English, therefore, assembled and returned at a good pace to Calais, where they revelled that night and talked amongst themselves of the feats that had been done. The French returned also to Saint Inghelberth; and if the English talked of the things that had fallen out that day, you may believe that the French did the same.

Of the Second Day.

The Tuesday, after mass and a morning draught, all those who wished to see the jousts, with those who were to tilt, came out of Calais and rode together in a company, with great order, to the place of arms; and when they were come, the French were ready to receive them, as was right. The day was bright and clear, and warm enough. The English drew up in order and armed those who were to joust.

After many courses had been well and bravely performed without accident, there stepped forward a young knight named Sir Godfrey Seton, known as a good tilter and showing it by his manner of riding and carrying his lance. He sent a squire to touch the war-shield of Sir Regnault de Roye, who readily answered. The two knights spurred at the same moment as straight as arrows, and met, striking each other such blows on their shields that though the lances did not break by reason of their toughness, yet they remained fixed in the shields, and by dint of hard pushing the horses were stopped, and the knights returned to their places without losing their lances, but carrying them fairly before them, and then laying them in fest. Then spurring their horses again, which were good ones, young and strong, they met again, but not straight, by the fault of the horses, not of the knights themselves, and in passing they lost their lances. Those standing by picked them up and gave them to them, and as soon as they had received them they couched them and returned to the encounter, for they were heated and would not spare themselves. The English knight struck Sir Regnault a heavy blow on the upper part of his helmet, but did not hurt him; and in return Sir Regnault, who was at that time one of the strongest and toughest tilters in France, being smitten with love for a gay and beautiful young lady, which was a great help to him in all his affairs, gave him a blow on the shield so severe that it pierced it and his arm as well. The lance was broken and the butt end fell to the ground, the upper end remaining fixed in the shield and the steel in the arm. For all this the knight finished his course very handsomely, and returned to his place. His companions came to him, and the splinter and steel were drawn out, and the blood staunched and the wound bound up. Sir Regnault returned to his place, and remained leaning on a spear which was given him. He was much praised by his own party, nor did the English say any harm of him, although his adversary had been hurt; for such is the fortune of arms—to one good, to another evil; and certainly they tilted without sparing one another.

Then, after several English knights had run their courses with honour, there came forward a young knight named Thomalin Messidon, well armed and in good disposition for fighting, and challenged Sir Boucicault, who was ready. In the first course they struck one another on the helms, and passed on without any accident or damage. They returned to their places, and spurred again to the charge, and in this course they met, striking one another with great violence on the shields. The spear of Sir Thomalin broke into splinters, but Sir Boucicault's blow was so strong that he carried his opponent to the ground over the tail of his horse. Those on his side came and lifted him up and led him away, and he tilted no more that day.

The tilting went on till it grew late and near the time for vespers, and then the English drew together as they had done before, and returned in a company to Calais, and the French to St. Inghelberth.

You must know, although I have made no mention of it as yet, that King Charles of France greatly desired to see these jousts, for at that time he was very lively and loved much to see new things. It was told me that he was present from the first to the last, but in disguise, so that no man knew it save the Lord de Garencières, who came with him and was also disguised, and the two returned each day to Marquise.

Of the Third Day.

So Tuesday passed, and Wednesday came, and it was a very fine day, like the preceding one. The English mounted again on horseback after mass and the morning draught, and came out of Calais in great order, and rode along the road of Sangate till they came to the place where the French were rejoiced to receive them.

As soon as the English were come they lost no time, and a squire named John Savage, a good tilter, squire of the body to the Earl of Huntingdon, sent to touch the shield of Sir Regnault. They met with great violence, striking one another full on the middle of the shield so forcibly that both would have fallen to the ground if the shields had not given way. This was a first and perilous course, though the tilters received no hurt, for the lances passed through the targets and slipped off the side armour breaking about a foot from the shaft, and the upper end remaining in the shield, and the knights held the shafts before them while they finished the course. Those who saw doubted not that they were severely hurt, and each side surrounded their champion. But when they found they were not touched they were greatly rejoiced, and told them they had done enough for that day. But this did not satisfy John Savage, and he said that he had not crossed the sea to break but one single lance. These words were carried to Sir Regnault de Roye, who answered, 'He is right, and he ought to be gratified, either by me or by my companions.'

Therefore they returned to their places and obtained fresh spears and shields. Then spurring, as they drew near they lowered their spears and endeavoured to meet fairly, but could not, for their horses swerved. So the second course failed, to their great rage. Then having received their lances, which they had dropped, they placed them in rest, and in the third career they struck each other full on the visors of the helmets, so that in passing they were unhelmed. It was a fine course, and won great praise. Then the

English came and told John Savage that he had done very well, and it was now time for him to make way for others. To this he agreed, and laid aside lance and shield, and dismounted from his charger, taking instead a hackney, which he mounted to see the rest of the jousts.

Then after two more Englishmen had run their courses with the French knights with honour, and a third had been overthrown in tilting with the Lord de Saint-Py, there came forward Sir John Arundel, who was a good knight and renowned both in tilting, dancing, and singing, and who was young and full of courage, and sent to challenge the knight, Sir Regnault de Roye. They spurred against one another with good will, and gave great blows, but neither fell, though they lost their lances. In the second course they struck full upon the helms, so that the sparks flew, but no damage was done. In the third the horses swerved and they dropped their lances. The fourth blow struck the helmets, but neither was unhelmed; and the fifth the shields, breaking both the spears, and still without damage to the knights. So the tilting went on that day as before, and in the evening they separated again.

Of the Fourth Day.

And on the morning of Thursday the English looked to see who amongst them there were who had yet to do the feats of arms for which they had come over the sea, and they agreed that such should be satisfied, as was fitting. Therefore they mounted again and returned to Saint Inghelberth, where they found the French knights ready and waiting in their pavilions. Many fine courses were run; and at length a knight of Bohemia, of the retinue of the Queen of England, whom they called Herr Hans, sent to challenge Sir Boucicault. They spurred with great good will, but failed to meet fairly, owing to the ill conduct of the Bohemian, who, out of the line of tilting, struck Sir Boucicault on the helmet and continued his course. He was greatly blamed, and the English saw that he had forfeited both arms and horse if the French insisted on it. They held a long conversation about this, but at last the French pardoned him, the better to please the English. Herr Hans begged as a favour that he might be allowed to run one course more. They asked him, 'With whom?' He sent to say, 'Sir Regnault de Roye.' The knight, who had done nothing yet that day, replied that he was willing. They met, striking in the centre of the shields, and Sir Regnault, who was one of the best and strongest tilters of his time, struck him in such a manner that he flew clean out of his stirrups and fell so heavily on the earth that they thought he was dead. Herr Hans was raised by his people and carried away. The English were well pleased that it had so happened because of the uncourteous manner in which he had run his first course, and you may be sure he had no wish to do any more that day.

After other English squires had run their courses, there came forward another,—a fine man, tall and

straight, sitting his horse well, fully armed for tilting.
His name was Jacquemin Scrope. He sent to touch
the shield of the Lord de Saint-Py. They laid lance
in rest and came against one another with great good-
will ; but the first blow missed, for their horses crossed,
which angered them greatly ; and they returned to
their positions, and without delay spurring their horses,
lowering their lances, met again and struck one
another a blow so hard on the helmet that sparks flew
out. They passed on, for the lances did not remain
fixed but flew into shivers. They received fresh
lances and met again with great violence, striking
each the other's shield with great force. The lance
of Jacquemin was broken, but Saint-Py used his well,
for he struck the squire so hard that he threw him
from his saddle. He did no more that day, being
raised from the ground by his people.

After two more English squires had run their
courses with Sir Boucicault and the Lord de Saint-
Py, the jousts ceased for that day, nor did any more
advance from that party.

Then the Earl of Huntingdon, the Earl Marshal,
the Lord Clifford, and all the other knights who
had jousted during these four days, came to the
French knights and gave them great thanks for
the pastime, saying to them, 'All the knights and
squires who desired to joust have done so. Now,
therefore, we take leave of you, for we return to
Calais, and from thence to England. We know
well that whosoever wishes to tilt with you will find
you here throughout the thirty days, according to

the tenor of your proclamation. When we be come to England, we certify you, we will tell all such as shall meet and speak with us on this matter and pray them that they come to see you.'

'We thank you greatly,' replied the three knights, 'they shall be gladly welcome, and shall be delivered of their vow, as you have been. And withal, we return you hearty thanks for the courtesy you have done us.'

Thus peaceably and gently did the English depart from St. Inghelberth and return to Calais. They stayed there not long,—on Saturday, in the morning, they went on board the passage-boats. The wind was fair, and before noon they came to Dover. Then they came from the vessels and came into the town, each going to his inn. Thus they passed the Saturday and Sunday, till mass was over, at Dover, and rested themselves and their horses; but they lay on Sunday at Rochester, coming the next day to London. There they took leave of one another and returned each to his home. Meanwhile, the knights of France remained at their posts at St. Inghelberth.

You shall know, as I said above, that when the English had bidden the French knights farewell, the King of France and the Lord de Garencières, who had been there disguised and had witnessed the feats of arms, left, and lay that night at Marquise, and the next day they returned to France and never ceased riding till they came to Cray, on the river Oise, where the Queen held her court at that time. Few knew where the King had been, save his most trusty body-servant.

After that company of English of whom I have told you had returned into England, I could never hear that any other came out of that country to joust at St. Inghelberth. Nevertheless the three knights above named remained at that place for the full thirty days and more, and then returned at their ease each to his home, after that they had gone to see the King of France, the Duke of Touraine, and the lords at Paris, who made them good cheer, as was right, for they had borne themselves valiantly and had well maintained the honour of the realm of France.

CHAPTER XII.

THE LAST DEEDS OF SIR HARRY HOTSPUR.

Of Owen Glendower and the Earl Douglas.

Now it came to pass that the Welsh, taking advantage of the King's absence, rose in rebellion, having as their leader a certain Owen Glendower. He had been first apprenticed to the law at Westminster, and then became esquire to the late king; and had fought with honour, but a quarrel having arisen between him and Lord Reginald Grey de Ruthyn, on account of lands which he claimed as his inheritance, on grounds of little weight, he took up arms, first against Lord Grey, wasting his lands with fire and sword, so that many perished cruelly. Which when the King heard he marched straightway against the disturber of the peace of the country, and having collected a multitude of armed men and archers, invaded Wales. But the Welsh with their leader retreating to Mount Snowden, escaped the threatened vengeance. So the King, having burnt the country and put to death all whom fate brought within reach of his sword, returned with little spoil of horses and cattle into England.

And in the month of March there appeared in the north-west a comet, shooting out terrible flames to a great height, turning at last towards the north, where it ceased to be seen, signifying, as it was thought, that much blood would be shed in those parts where it appeared, that is, Wales and Northumberland.

And, again, Owen Glendower, with a band of Welshmen, ravaged the country, carrying some away captive and putting others to a cruel death. And he wasted the lands of Lord Reginald Grey, who was at that time dwelling in his castle of Ruthyn, and he, hearing of his coming, went out against him with few men, hoping to be able to capture him. But it fell not out as he hoped, for when they fought together Lord de Grey was taken, and many of his men killed. And this disaster increased the pride of the Welsh, and made their madness greater, as will be seen. Then Owen Glendower challenged the men of Hereford to battle, and they went out to meet him, under Edmund Mortimer, the most valiant of those parts, fearing nothing but the flight of the Cambrians. But alas! by treachery those who hastened to conquer were unexpectedly overthrown, and more than eleven hundred of our men were killed and Edmund Mortimer was taken, and with him some knights and armed men and servants, whose names I know not. And such deeds were perpetrated as were unheard of in any age, neither would they suffer the bodies of the dead to be buried without a heavy fine and ransom. There are those who say that Edmund Mortimer was captured by agreement and premeditated treason, and this opinion the infamous intercourse of Edmund with Owen afterwards greatly confirmed.

Then the King of England, about the Feast of the Assumption, having gathered troops, entered Wales, giving one army to his son the Prince and another to the Earl of Arundel, having with him a third, so that entering secretly they might enclose Owen Glendower and his confederates with less chance of escape. But so much din of arms availed nothing, for the Welsh hid in new hiding-places; and the King suffered much, it was supposed from magical devices, and also the army which he led; for from the day in which he entered the borders of Cambria to that on which he left the place, the air was never serene, but day and night rain, mixed with snow and hail, so afflicted the army that they could not endure the excessive cold. And on the vigil of the Nativity of the Blessed Virgin, when the King had fixed his tent in a pleasant meadow, where from the nature of the place they feared nothing, but hoped for quiet repose, suddenly, in the first watch of the night, there came down such an abundance of water that the English were nearly overwhelmed by it. There came also such a tempest of wind that it tore and blew down the tent of the King himself, and threw down the King's lance, driving it into the armour of the King with such force that it would have been the King's last night if he had not slept armed. Nor did those English, who were used of old to war, remember to have been ever so much vexed and exposed to peril, in any expedition that they had seen, without human agency. Whence many are of opinion, if it is lawful to believe it, that these evil arts were devised by the Minor Friars, who were said to favour the Welsh party. But far be it from men of such a holy profession to hold familiar intercourse with devils, and bring upon their glory a stain never to be wiped off. Nevertheless the King, forced by necessity, returned to his burnt lands, sad at these disasters.

Then, at the same time, the haughty Scots, growing bold during the absence of the King in Wales, and thinking none were left in the country to stop their course, with a numerous army in great array under Earl Douglas, entered the eastern part of Northumberland. But being warned of their coming, the Earl of Northumberland secretly collected an army, and he permitted the Scots to enter and rage in their usual way, hoping, as it fell out, to stop the way as they returned, and force them either to give battle or take to flight. Nor did this stratagem fail, for when the Scots learned that those whom they least expected to see, the Earl and Henry Percy, his son, and the Earl of Dunbar (who not long before leaving the Scots had sworn faith to England), were in arms against them, they made haste to retreat. For they had supposed all these to have been gone into Wales, carrying aid to the King. So they turned their bridles towards their own land, labouring to reach roads which lead to Scotland before the Earl. But the Earl and his men, riding all the night, came to the place by which they must pass, and with his army gathered in the valley waited for their coming. The morning having come, the Scots, thinking that the Earl had been left behind, rode on with all speed lest the English should overtake them. But avoiding Scylla they fell into Charybdis, for they found those whom they thought to have escaped in well-ordered array before them. They were forced to stand and prepare for battle, so they chose a hill near the place. And our men, therefore, seeing them take possession of the hill, occupied the other hill themselves, and the valley separated them. It was a fair sight to see; on this side the English excellently armed, with their archers, and on that the Scots, with their bowmen, trusting in their armour, which being like silver reflected back the rays of the sun. Now there were returning from an expedition a troop of five hundred bowmen, who had gone out that night seeking victuals, and seeing the two armies with their standards unfurled on the two hills, they themselves being suddenly between them, they sent out a certain number of their archers, who shot at the Scots and provoked them to descend. Then there came out some of the Scots, and the archers retired before them, but our men coming up, the Scotch archers were forced to turn their backs. But their courage did not fail them, and they essayed to shoot upon our men, till the raining tempest of our arrows put them to flight. Then Earl Douglas, seeing his men flee, determined to show them that he was not deserting the battle, so he, with a company of knights, trusting in the strength of their armour, lowered their lances and descended impetuously to attack the archers. But when the bowmen saw him they went backward, shooting their arrows more thickly, and the arrows penetrated the armour everywhere, and pierced the helmets and the swords, and split the lances. And Douglas himself was wounded in five places, in spite of his strong and sumptuous armour. Then the rest of the Scots who had not descended from the mountain turned round and prepared to flee, but all who fell into the hands of the archers were captured or slain, and among them Earl Douglas was taken. And some fleeing with great speed came to the river of Tweed, and not knowing the fords were by the strength of the current carried away and drowned, to the number of five hundred, as it is asserted. But God be praised for all, for He gave us the victory, not by the leaders and captains, but through the poor and the servants, neither was there a lord, nor a knight, nor an armed man, who moved a foot against the Scots, but they were overthrown by the archers, as I have said.

Now the young Edmund Mortimer, who had been captured by Owen Glendower, either from weariness of captivity, or fear of death, or some other cause unknown, declared himself for Owen against the King of England, and contracted a marriage, unworthy of his noble race, with Owen's daughter. It is said that at the birth of Glendower there occurred fearful and prodigious things, for in the morning his father's horses were found standing in their stable deep in blood, which many thought to forebode evil things.

And Lord Reginald de Grey, by payment of a ransom of ten thousand marks, was set free.

Then the following summer, near the towns of Bedford and Biggleswade, there were seen frequently in the morning and at midday monsters coming out of the woods, of various colours, in the appearance of men-of-war, fighting together and beginning a hard battle. But though they could be seen at a distance, they could not be found on approaching the place. And this fantastical apparition deceived many, so that they went to look.

And the Earl of Northumberland, with his son, making an expedition into Scotland, devastated the country, carrying away captives and spoil with no resistance. But when he was returned, a rumour went through all England that the Scots were prepared for war at the feast of St. Peter ad Vincula. For the Earl had laid siege to a certain castle in the expedition, and when he attacked it vehemently, the besieged, it is said, prayed for a truce until that feast, on which day, if the Scots did not give battle, or if he won the victory, they would give up the castle to him. At this rumour all the youth of England, and the nobility of the kingdom, and the King himself, bestirred themselves, hoping to be present at the battle. But the Earl showed the King that it was not a work that needed his presence, but that he should remain quiet and barons gather together. But while many made ready for this business, it was shown to be naught but an idle fancy.

Of Henry Percy and Shrewsbury Field.

About that time Lord Henry Percy the younger, whom fortune had greatly favoured hitherto in deeds of war, in the esteem of the common people, and in temporal things, suddenly, with many confederates, declared himself against the King of England, and gathered an army near Shrewsbury, hoping, it is supposed, for the aid of Owen Glendower and Edmund Mortimer, and the archers and men-at-arms of Chester and Wales. Lord Thomas Percy, his uncle, earl of Worcester (whom the King had made guardian and governor of his eldest son, the Prince of Wales), secretly encouraged him, and gave him assistance by withdrawing his treasure from London and from the house of the Prince. And he himself joined his nephew Henry with what men he could bring. And they, to excuse themselves for their conspiracy, wrote letters to diverse leaders and people of the kingdom, asserting that their purpose was not against the allegiance and fidelity that they owed to the King, neither had they assembled the army for any other end but for the security of their persons, and that they might reform the public abuses. And they wrote also that the taxes, given to the King for the safe-keeping of the kingdom, were not put to the right uses, but devoured and consumed uselessly; on which account they felt themselves bound, for the good of the country, to assemble men, that they might provide a remedy for the evil.

Many then praised their insolence and extolled the faith which they pretended to the country. But the King knew their falseness, and, with a troubled mind, he considered how he could satisfy the people and confound their devices. So he wrote letters, saying that he wondered greatly that, when the Earl of Northumberland and his son Henry had received the greatest part of the sums conceded for keeping the Marches of Scotland, as he could evidently show, they should find cause for so much complaint and manifest detraction. He wrote, moreover, that he knew that the Earl of Northumberland and his son Henry, and the Earl of Worcester also, had certified to many by letters that, on account of the evil information and secret accusations of their rivals, the King was so much moved against them that they dared not come into his presence. Therefore he wrote to the Earl and Henry, that if they would they might come to him safely and depart in safety, without deceit or peril. But Hotspur would listen to no reason, nor stop to think, and, despising the royal lenity, armed himself for rebellion, and hastened to Shrewsbury. Then the King, when he perceived the determined malice of the youth (for his father did not leave the borders of his lands), determined immediately to encounter Henry and his uncle, Lord Thomas Percy, earl of Worcester, before they could raise an army against him.

Then their party caused it to be published through the kingdom that King Richard **was** still alive and was among them, and that they made war in his

name against King Henry; and if any desired to see
him they should come in arms to them, and that in
the castle of Chester they would certainly find the
King. By this crafty proclamation they moved the
minds of many to waver, not knowing to which party
they might safely adhere; for King Richard had
power over many in those times, especially over those
who had been familiar with him, and had received
from him fiefs or other gifts.

Then King Henry, being bold of mind and prompt
in action, assembled all whom he could and betook
himself to the place where the rebels Henry and the
Earl were known to be. The Earl of Dunbar, a Scot,
urged him not to delay, for he said, 'If thou waitest
in London, or near London, his forces will grow daily
in the remote counties, and then it will be necessary
to yield to them whatever they may. I say not sup-
plicate, but command.' And when the King urged
that he had not sufficient troops, 'Care not for numbers,' he answered, 'but advance cautiously against
them, and then you will be able to see with your own
eyes who love you from their hearts and who are
feigning.' And the King did as the Scot advised, and
came unexpectedly to the place where the rebels were
revelling. When Henry Percy saw his standard he
was astonished above measure, for he thought him to
have tarried at the town of Burton-upon-Trent, waiting the coming of his counsellors; and therefore, because he had no suspicion of the coming of the King,
he had laid siege to the town of Shrewsbury, demanding that they should give him entrance that he might

refresh himself and provide victuals for his army. But the coming of the King was very advantageous for the men of Shrewsbury, for when he saw the standard of the King, Henry immediately left off troubling the citizens, saying to his men, 'Comrades and fellow-soldiers, we must give up this enterprise and turn our arms against those who are coming with the King. You see the King's standard, therefore be wise men; for this day will either advance us all if you determine to remain with me, or we shall meet our ruin.'

Then all those who were with Henry, to the number of fourteen thousand chosen men, agreed with one voice that they would stand by him. And they chose the ground very convenient for them; for it was necessary for the King's army, if they wished to join battle, to advance over ground sown with peas; and they bound together and entangled the peas, so that they were like snares to those who advanced. And when Henry saw that they were without doubt about to fight, and that the sword he loved best was missing, he sought it everywhere: and they told him that it was in the little town behind, commonly called Berwick. And at that word he turned pale, so that those standing by marvelled; then, drawing a deep sigh, he said to his servant, 'I perceive that my plough is at its last furrow, for it was prophesied to me when I was yet in my own country that I should without doubt die at Berwick. But, alas! the name deceived me.' Then he ordered the battle wisely, promising his followers an end of their troubles that day, if they survived, and riches, and a glorious future, and a name for ever.

And of the nobles who followed him to that place there were his uncle, Lord Thomas Percy, earl of Worcester, who was never before in all his life suspected of perfidy, and who alone among the English, who are known abroad for their fickleness, obtained praise for faithfulness, so that the kings of France and Spain trusted his word more than any writing; and Earl Douglas, the Scot, had followed him, who had been captured in the battle of Homildon Hill, and he was a very warlike man and equalled by few for courage, prudence, or fortitude. And the Lord Kinderton, and Sir Hugh Browne, and also Sir Richard Vernon, were there, with ten other barons.

Then the King, perceiving the order of the army opposed to him, and chiefly the archers gathered together, ordered his own army with the alacrity that became him; and committing part to his eldest son the Prince, retained another part under his own command. The front of the King's battle was given to the Earl of Stafford, a man of great honour, who was that day made Constable of the Kingdom. And when each army was opposed to the other and waiting the signal for battle, the Abbot of Shrewsbury and the Clerk of the Privy Seal went to Henry on the part of the King, offering him peace if he would desist from his undertaking, demanding to know his grievances and those of them that were with him, which they promised on the part of the King should be redressed, if he would refer them to arbitration. If he would secretly explain them to the King, they prayed him to send one whom he could trust to go with them to the King and lay his wishes before him, who, God willing, would bring him back good tidings.

Henry, somewhat moved by these persuasions, sent his uncle, Lord Thomas Percy, to the King, that he should explain to him the cause of the trouble and demand redress. And some say that the King agreed to all the matters, but that Lord Thomas, when he returned to his nephew, perverted the business, bringing back a contrary answer, and exasperating the young man and urging him to battle against his will. With such embassies much of the day passed away, and it was told the King that the rebels delayed the negotiations only that their allies might come up on the next Monday and strengthen them. And it was Saturday when these things were done. Then the Earl of Dunbar urged him to delay no longer, but to give the signal for battle.

From the other side, as soon as the messengers had reached their own camp, Henry's archers began to shoot their arrows—and better men could not be found in the county of Chester—and many of the King's men fell by them; and there was made such a slaughter that four thousand of the King's army took to flight, thinking that, without doubt, the King was shot. Then the leader of the rebels and the Earl Douglas, than whom none were found bolder, despising the arrows of the King's archers and the body of armed men, turned their arms towards one person alone—to wit, the King—esteeming him worth

Here shewes howe at the batell of Shrewesbury
bettwen kyng henr the iiij{th} & sr henr percy/
there was slayne the said sr henr percy
and many other w{t} hym And on the kyngs p{ar}ty
there was slayne the Erle of Stafford w{t} many
other in grett nombre

ten thousand, seeking him with lances lowered and drawn swords. But the Earl of Dunbar, perceiving their purpose, drew the King away, lest his pursuers should find out where he was ; which change of place was very fortunate for the King, for his standard-bearer was overthrown and his standard thrown down and torn, and those who were round it killed, among whom were the brave young Earl of Stafford and Sir Walter Blunt.

In the meantime many fell in both armies, shot by chance arrows, which flew as thick as hail; and the Prince, now for the first time in battle, was wounded in the face by an arrow: but though he was but a youth, he quailed not, but making light of the wound, encouraged the army to stand firm. And the men committed to him were the first to reach the enemy's lines, and they penetrated them and passed through them, overthrowing all who opposed, so that they were shut in between the Prince's men and the squadron of the King. And the enemy were in doubt, not knowing whether they were fighting against the King's men or their own companions.

At this time of confusion their leader, Henry Percy, fell slain, by whose hand is not known, his men not knowing of his fall, but supposing him either to have taken the King or to have killed him. Therefore, to encourage themselves, they cried again and again, ' Henry Percy, king!' which the King hearing, that they might not fight longer, because of their vain hopes, desiring to prevent more bloodshed, cried as loud as he could, ' Henry Percy is dead!' And when they heard that, even those who were fighting most earnestly, began to draw off, and to see their only hope in flight. And the King's men gaining courage, there were slain a great part of the knights of the county of Chester, to the number, it is said, of two hundred. And there fell besides of foot-soldiers and servants a great number, I know not how many; and Earl Douglas was taken. But if the rest of the rebels had imitated his courage and constancy, there is no doubt that an incurable wound would have been made in the kingdom of England. Thus, twice in that year fighting against the English, he found fortune adverse; for in the first battle he lost an eye and was taken prisoner, and in the second he was grievously wounded and again made prisoner. And the Earl of Worcester, Thomas Percy, was also taken prisoner; and he, it was said, was the stirrer-up of all the evil, and the cause of the disaster. And Sir Richard Vernon was captured, and the Lord Kinderton, both noble and powerful men.

On the King's side there fell the Earl of Stafford, Sir John Clifton, Sir Walter Blunt, Sir B. Gousile, and many more. And this Sir B. Gousile, who had that day been made a knight, was not slain in battle, but fell by the treachery of one of his own household, as he was retiring from the battle wounded in the side. For as he threw himself down under a hedge, seeming about to draw his last breath, there came one of his household, to whom he had shown much love. He had fled at the beginning of the battle, but returned when the battle was over, that in the evening he might spoil the dead, as the manner is of such people. And, alone, he came to the place where his lord was lying, and he knew him by his arms. And when he was come, he asked his lord how he was. And he, as well as he was able, answered, that he was alive, but much weighed down. 'I am suffocated by my armour; take off my breastplate and arms, that I may revive.' Therefore, when the breastplate was removed, he gave him a ring to carry to his wife, and told him that he had sixty marks in a box, which he commanded him to keep for him if he lived, but that if he died he might take them for his own use. But what would a traitor do who had deserted his master? The coward in battle drove his knife into his master's uncovered breast, and held him till he saw that he was quite dead. Then he took his collar, and rings, and jewels, and all the marks of his nobility, and the money, and went away, leaving his master's naked body lying under the hedge. But a certain soldier saw and heard it all; for he was escaped from the field of battle, crawling on his hands and knees to the same hedge, being revived by the fresh air, for he was himself wounded and overpowered by the weight of his armour. So he afterwards made known the wickedness of the ruffian, telling it all to his mistress when he recovered. She was the Duchess of Norfolk, widow of the Duke, Lord Thomas Mowbray, who died in exile. And the villain being found by the things he had stolen, suffered the due penalty of his deeds.

Of the common people who died on the King's side

the number was not given, but of the wounded there were three thousand, of whom the greater part died afterwards. This battle was fought on Saturday, the vigil of St. Mary Magdalene, in the afternoon, and those who were there say that there was never a fiercer, for there were many on both sides fighting so steadfastly that when night came they did not know whose was the victory, and they lay mingled together weary, wounded, and bleeding.

The next day the King commanded the bodies of the dead to be buried; and when he saw the body of Henry Percy it is said he wept, protesting he was grieved by his death. And as there were many who would not believe him dead, he ordered that his body should be exposed that all might see him. Then many sent mediators to the King to plead with him; and Thomas Percy, earl of Worcester, when he saw the body of his nephew, shed abundance of tears, saying he cared not what fortune might do for him. The following Monday, by judicial sentence, he was beheaded, although the King, it is said, wished to spare his life, but he had much enraged the King's friends; and with him were beheaded Lord Kinderton and Sir Richard Vernon.

Then the Earl of Northumberland, with a strong force, hastening to his son, or, as some say, to the King to make peace, heard that the Earl of Westmoreland and Robert Waterton had assembled a great army to oppose him if he advanced further; and he turned rein and came to Newcastle upon Tyne, and the citizens, seeing the army following him, closed the gates against him. But he prayed for entrance to rest there that night, and the citizens replied that he might enter with his family, but on no account with an army; and the Earl, accepting the conditions, entered the town, and stayed there that night and the next day with few companions, but the army, being excluded, either from desire of vengeance or fear of their master the Earl being betrayed, came to the walls and tried to enter the town by force. But it availed them nothing, for they were repulsed by the archers and wounded. Then the Earl satisfied them as well as he could, and, excusing himself to the citizens, went away, and when he heard of his son's death he dismissed his army and retired with his family to his own castle of Warkworth.

And the King came to York to meet the Earl in battle if he would not submit and send away his army, and when he heard of his coming he sent letters to him, and the Earl came to him with few attendants on the morrow after Saint Lawrence; but he was received neither with joy nor kindness as he was wont to be, but as a suppliant seeking favour; and in few words the King promised him life and honourable treatment, but he gave him not his liberty, but kept him under guard until the time appointed.

CHAPTER XIII.

KING HENRY V. IN FRANCE.

Of the Siege of Harfleur.

OUR intrepid and magnanimous Prince having set the kingdom of England in order, went on board his ship the *Trinity*, between Southampton and Portsmouth, and gave command that the sail should be hoisted that all the ships might assemble; and when they were all gathered together, in number about fifteen hundred, he set sail with a favourable wind: and when they had passed the Isle of Wight there came some swans and swam in the midst of the ships, and all said it was a happy omen. Then the next day, about the hour of noon, they entered the river of Seine, which flows from Paris to the sea by Rouen and Harfleur, and they cast anchor at a place called Chefde Caux, about three miles from Harfleur. But the King forbade any to land that night. Then the next morning, before daybreak, Sir John Holland, earl of Huntingdon, went with certain horsemen to reconnoitre the place, and afterwards, when the morning dawned and the sun shone clear, the King, with the chief part of his army, came to land in little boats and skiffs, and took up their position on a little hill near Harfleur, having on one side a wood going down to the river of Seine, and on the other farms and orchards. The shore, being covered with rough stones, was perilous for landing, and the enemy had made in one part a deep ditch, and fortified it with mud walls up to the marsh, which is very dangerous, but they left it now undefended, although with but few men they might have opposed many thousands.

Then the King caused it to be proclaimed in the camp that none, under pain of death, should set fire to any building, nor injure or destroy any church or sacred place; neither should they lay hands on any priest or woman; and, dividing his army into three parts, he moved against the town, appearing on the hill over against it, for on the other side he could not approach it on account of the tide and the stream flowing through the valley. For the town is situated at the end of a valley at the mouth of the Seine, and the sea at high tide rises to the town. A stream of fresh water fills the deep and wide ditches outside the walls to the bank of the river, which enters under the walls by a watergate and two arches, which the inhabitants can open and close at their pleasure. And the town was surrounded by walls with high towers, and it had three gates, before each of which the enemy had erected a defence called a barbican, with great trees bound strongly together as high nearly as the walls of the town. It was built round in form, and had many chinks and crevices through which they could shoot upon us with arrows and darts, or with their tubes, which we in English call 'gunnys.' All round about was deep water, two lances' length in breadth at the narrowest part, with a little bridge that they could draw up and down at will.

Ships could come up into the middle of the town, and the harbour had walls with two fine towers at the entrance, armed and fortified; but the enemy had planted stakes in the water at the entrance to hinder our ships from coming in. And the town had many fine buildings and one parish church.

And the army, having taken up its position before the town in the fields and orchards, the King gave care to the providing of victuals for man and beast, and for guarding the camp from attack. But the other side of the town being left open, the next day the Lord de Gaucort entered the town with three hundred lances, being sent to aid the defence. Therefore the King sent Thomas, duke of Clarence, with part of the army, to press the siege on that side; but the march was difficult and dangerous, for the town had broken down the bridges and caused the stream to flood the valley, that it was wider than the Thames at London. And on his way he captured great store of guns and powder, with crossbows and arrows, which were being carried to the town from the city of Rouen. And in the morning he took up his position on the hill on the other side, and the stream being guarded by boats and the entrance from the sea by the King's ships, the siege was ordered all round the town.

Then the King sent to offer peace to the besieged, if they would open the gates to him and give up the town to him, the rightful Duke of Normandy. But they refusing to obey, the King set up his engines before the town, and built over them edifices of wood and iron, that the soldiers might be shielded from the missiles of the enemy, while they shot stones from the guns with ignited powder. And he directed his strongest attack against the barbican before the chief gate, battering it with stones and digging mines beneath it, until in a few days it was in great part broken down. But the enemy did us what damage they could with their guns and crossbows, and as the walls and towers were broken by day, they heaped up in the breach by night logs and tubs filled with earth, and heaped up sand and stones. And they built up mounds of thick clay, into which the stones from the guns should sink, doing little harm. And they had vessels full of quick-lime and boiling oil to pour upon the heads of our men if they should approach too near.

The King began to construct great mines to undermine the walls, but being begun in sight of the enemy they frustrated them by counter-mines, and the fagots that were brought to fill up the ditches they set on fire and burnt.

And at this time there fell sick the Lord Richard Courtenay, bishop of Norwich, who was much beloved by the King, and in short space he died, the King himself closing his eyes, and sending his body to England to be buried at Westminster. The same day the enemy making a sortie did much damage to our men. But on the morrow the Earl of Huntingdon with his men set the barbican on fire, and took it.

Then the King caused it to be proclaimed by trumpet through the camp that all should prepare to storm the city and mount the walls, and that the next morning all the soldiers and the sailors from the ships should be in the places assigned to them by their captains. And that night he assailed the town more fiercely with stones from the guns, that the besieged might not have sleep or rest.

But the enemy, fearing the assault and despairing of succour, sent to pray for a truce, promising to give up the town if they were not rescued by the French King or the Dauphin before the first hour after noon of the Sunday following. And to this the King agreed. And the Bishop of Bangor, with all the King's chaplains, marching in procession in their hoods, carried the host to a place under the walls, and there they swore to the covenant; and twenty-three hostages were given up to the King, and a soldier sent to the French King. And the same day there died that noble soldier, the Lord Michael Pole, earl of Suffolk.

Then when within the time appointed there came none from the French King, nor from the Dauphin, to succour the city, the King, clad in gold and splendid raiment, being seated on his throne in a pavilion on the hill, his nobles and his captains standing by, and Sir Gilbert Umfraville on his right, bearing on a spear the crowned helmet of the King, the Lord de Gaucourt, with all who had sworn to the treaty, came before him and yielded up the keys of the city to him; and he received him graciously, and brought him and those that were with him, and the hostages, into his tent, and entertained them magnificently with what dainties he had.

And the banners of St. George and the King being set on the gates, the King made Thomas Beaufort, earl of Dorset, captain of the town And the Lord de Gaucourt, with the knights and nobles, were suffered to depart, having taken an oath to surrender themselves at Calais at the feast of Saint Martin. And the poor, with the women and children, were sent away to go where they would in France, being conducted by a body of armed men that they might not suffer harm at the hands of freebooters.

Then King Henry sent a herald to the Dauphin, challenging him to make an end of the quarrel between them by single combat. But having tarried at Harfleur the set time, and the Dauphin not replying, he put captains and soldiers in the town and made ready to march to Calais. But many of his men being sick, he permitted them to return to England; and great numbers having died by the sickness, besides those which had fallen by the sword, there remained with him but nine hundred spearmen and five thousand archers.

Q

How the King marched through the Land.

Then, having given command to his men to carry with them victuals for eight days, he set forth. And leaving the town of Monstre de Villiers on our right, we came on the Friday to the town of Arques, three miles from Dieppe, and they shot stones at us; but the King made a treaty with them, and they gave us free passage through the town and bread and wine. And the next day we came to Eu and passed it on our left hand; and some of the French army having assembled, fell upon us, but we drove them away. And the prisoners reported that the French army would fall upon us at the river of Somme. On the morrow (Sunday) we came to the town of Abbeville; and the advanced guard brought word to us that the bridges were broken down and the French army was gathered together on the other bank. Then we turned and marched up the river-bank to another crossing; but there also the causeways were broken, and the French assembled in great numbers. Then we feared greatly that our victuals would be consumed, and that the enemy would fall upon us when we were weak and faint for want of food; and thus, with many lamentations and prayers for deliverance, we went on our way towards the head of the river, leaving on one side the city of Amiens. And we came to a village of the Duke of Burgundy's, named Boves, and having parleyed with them, they gave us bread and wine to redeem their town and vineyards from being burnt.

And passing Corbie, the French came out and attacked us; but we made them fly, having captured two of them and killed others.

There was brought to the King at this time a soldier of the English army, who had stolen from a church a pix of copper gilt, thinking it to be gold, and by command of the King at the next village he was hanged.

Then the report being spread that the enemy would come with many horsemen to break through the line of the archers, the King gave command that each archer should carry with him a strong stake six feet in length, sharp at each end, that thus if the enemy attacked them they might drive the stake into the ground with one point inclined towards the enemy.

And when we came to Nesle, tidings were brought to the King that there was a ford over the river about a league distant, and coming to the spot we found two places where the water was little higher than to a horse's belly, but the approach to them was by long causeways, and the French had broken them in the middle, so that it was difficult to ride even in single file. Then Sir John Cornwall and Sir Gilbert Umfraville were sent across with their pennons and a body of spearmen and archers to guard the passage. And the King gave command to fill the breaches with fagots of wood and straw, so that three might ride abreast. Then he sent the baggage over by one ford and the soldiers by the other, standing himself at the entrance, lest the men in their eagerness should cause confusion. Thus the passage was made. But before a hundred of our men were over the French appeared in sight, and some horsemen rode hastily to the attack, but being repelled by the advanced guard, and seeing that a large part had by this time crossed and taken up a good position, they turned and rode away.

Now we began to cross about an hour after noon and the whole army had attained the other side in safety an hour before night, and we rejoiced greatly, trusting that the French would not now attack us. But the next day the Duke of Orleans and the Duke of Bourbon sent three heralds to bring the King word that they would fight with him before he came to Calais. Upon which the King, encouraging his men, prepared for battle the next day. But meeting with no resistance we came to the walled town of Peronne, and some French horsemen issued forth to attack us, but perceiving us to be ready they fled back to the town. And as we went on our way we beheld the road trodden by the French army, and it was as if there were many thousands gone before us. And we of the people, I speak not of the mighty ones, fearing the battle to be imminent, raised our eyes and hearts to heaven, crying aloud to God to have mercy on us, and in His great pity save us from the power of the French. And we went on and came to the river of Swords, and hearing that the enemy were on the other side we made haste to cross, and coming to the top of a hill we beheld before us in the valley the French army, in three companies, who halted about a mile from us, and filled the whole plain like an innumerable multitude of locusts.

Of the Battle of Agincourt.

Then our King immediately set us in array, cheering and encouraging his men with great intrepidity and graciousness, and all who had not done so before made their confession. And I heard a certain Sir Walter Hungerford lamenting in the King's presence that they had not another ten thousand of good English archers. But the King turning to him said, 'Thou speakest foolishly, for by the God of heaven, in Whose grace I trust, and in Whom I have a firm hope of victory, I would not have one more. Dost thou not believe that the Almighty with these few can overcome the pride of the French?'

Then the enemy, having considered us awhile, drew off to a field beyond a wood which lay on the left hand, on the road to Calais. Upon that the King advanced and followed them, but when the sun began to decline the French prepared to take up their position for the night in the orchards. And when darkness settled down upon us we could hear them calling to one another; but our King commanded us to keep silence, threatening if a gentleman should offend to take away his horse and harness, and if a servant that he should lose his left ear. And thus in silence we turned aside to a village, and took up our abode in some miserable houses and the gardens and orchards. And rain fell in abundance all that night. But the enemy perceiving our silence thought that we purposed to flee, and lighted fires, with strong guards to intercept us; and it is reported that they thought themselves so secure of us that they played at dice for our King and his nobles.

Then on the morrow, being the Feast of SS. Crispin and Crispinian, the 25th day of October, at break of day, the French formed in battle array, and took up their position in the field of Agincourt, through which went our road to Calais. Their vanguard was of footmen of their noblest and best, showing a forest of lances and shining helmets, and on each side was a company of horsemen to break the line of our archers. All the remainder, the rearguard and the wings, were on horseback, an innumerable multitude.

King Henry having heard mass, set his army in order, making but one line of battle, his vanguard, under the Duke of York, forming the right wing, and the rearguard, under the Lord de Camoys, the left, with a body of archers between them, the stakes being fixed in the ground to defend them from the horsemen.

But when the King saw that the French delayed to attack, and that the two armies had been face to face for many hours, he prepared to advance. And he gave command to carry the baggage to the rear, where were the priests praying earnestly for the King and his men. But as soon as the battle began the French plunderers fell upon them and carried away the sword and crown and many other precious things.

Then the King, crying to Heaven for aid, moved

SAYING MASS

towards the enemy, and I, sitting on horseback with the other priests in the rear, remembering what the Church at that time was reading, said in my heart, 'Remember us, O Lord! Our enemies are gathered together, glorying in their might. Shatter their strength and disperse them, that they may know that there is none other that fighteth for us, but only Thou, O God.'

And the two armies meeting, the French horsemen began to assail our archers; but by the rain of arrows they were compelled to give way, and fled to the rear. And the enemy's cross-bowmen, who were behind the armed men after the first hasty discharge, in which they wounded very few, also gave way and retreated. Then the French nobles, who were advancing in one body, either from fear of the arrows or hoping thus to prosper better, divided themselves into three bodies, and attacked in the three places where the standards were seen. And their attack was so fierce that they forced back our men almost a spear's length, at which we, fighting a priestly warfare, fell on our faces in bitterness of spirit, crying on God to remember us. And our men quickly recovered their strength, and the battle raged fiercely. And when their arrows were exhausted, catching up the stakes and the swords and lances which lay around them, the archers attacked and dispersed the enemy. Nor had the oldest men ever seen the English so daring and intrepid; but on the French fell a panic of fear, and some of the noblest of them surrendered more than ten times, but there was no leisure to make prisoners, and they were all cut down, and the multitude, coming on with undisciplined violence, fell down on the dead bodies before them, and were slaughtered as they lay. And where our standards were the dead lay heaped to the height of a man. Then, when the rest had taken flight, our men separated the living from the dead, proposing to keep them for ransom. But there rose a cry that the enemy's horsemen had gathered together again, and were coming upon our wearied men. Then all the prisoners were put to death without mercy, excepting the Dukes of Orleans and Bourbon and a very few others. But the enemy gave way at the King's approach, and left to us the bloody field, with their waggons and victuals, and stores of lances, arrows, and bolts.

And when the force of the enemy had been dispersed, and the battle was finished, we returned victorious through the heaps of slain. We could not refrain from grief and tears at the sight of so many soldiers, valiant and renowned when God was with them, who had sought their deaths at our hands. And if the sight awakened pity and compunction in us strangers, how much greater was the weeping and mourning of the people of the land! And truly I think there is no heart of flesh nor of stone that could have seen without tears the cruel deaths and bitter wounds of so many Christians.

And there fell of them the Dukes of Brabant, Bar, and Alençon, five earls, and more than ninety barons, a thousand five hundred knights, and between four and five thousand other nobles. And there were taken, besides the Dukes of Orleans and Bourbon, the Earls of Richemont, Vendôme, and Eu, with the Lord Boucicault, marshal of France, and a few others. But great was the joy and wonder of our men when they found that of our men had fallen but nine or ten with the noble Duke of York, and the young Lord Michael, earl of Suffolk. And Duke Humphrey of Gloucester, the King's brother, receiving as he gave to others, was grievously wounded in the King's company, but after his coming to Calais he recovered.

Then, after the battle was over, the King, having rested that night in the same spot as he did the night before, set out on his way to Calais, and he came to the place on the day after the Feast of St. Simon and St. Jude; and the Saturday after Martinmas the Lord de Gaucourt and the other captives of Harfleur having come to him, he returned into England and came to the port of Dover.

Of the Entry of the King into London.

And having rested there one day, he took his way by Canterbury to his manor of Eltham, proposing to enter his City of London on the following Saturday; and the citizens made great preparations to receive him worthily. And when the day was come they went out to Blackheath to meet him, the Mayor and twenty-three aldermen in scarlet, and the rest in red garments with red and white hoods. In all there were about twenty thousand horses, and they bore the signs of their several crafts. And about the tenth hour the King came to them; and when they had given thanks to God for his victory, and had congratulated him, they led the way back to the City, followed by the King with a small company.

And when they were come to the bridge, on the tower at the entrance was a great statue, bearing, like a champion, a great axe in his right hand and the keys of the city in his left; and on his left hand stood the statue of a woman clad in scarlet; and around were the royal banners, and the trumpets and clarions sounded, and beneath was written, '*Civitas Regis justitiæ.*' Then, as they passed along, they saw on each side a little tower, painted to look like marble and green jasper; and on one was an antelope with the royal sceptre in his right foot and the arms round his neck, and on the other a lion erect, bearing in his right claws the royal standard unfurled. Over the road was another tower, and beneath a splendid pavilion was a statue of St. George with a laurel-wreath studded with pearls, and on his right hung his helmet, and on his left his shield. And in a house near were a great number of boys dressed in white, like angels with glittering wings, who sang with sweet voices to the sound of organs the English canticle :—

> ' Deo gratias Anglia redde pro victoria !
> Our King went forth to Normandy,
> With grace and might of chivalry;
> The God for him wrought marvellously,
> Wherefore England may call and cry,
>   Deo gratias, &c.

He set a siege, the sooth for to say,
To Harfleur town, with royal array;
The town he won, and made a fray
That France shall rue till doomsday!
    Deo gratias, &c.

Then went our King with all his host
Through France, for all the French boast
He spared for dread of least nor most,
Till he come to Agincourt coast.
    Deo gratias, &c.

Then, forsooth, that knight comely,
In Agincourt field he fought manly;
Through grace of God most mighty,
He had both the field and the victory.
    Deo gratias, &c.

Their dukes and earls, lord and baron,
Were take and slain, and that well soon;
And some were led into London,
With joy, and mirth, and great renown!
    Deo gratias, &c.

Now, gracious God, He save our King,
His people, and all his well willing;
Give him good life, and good ending,
That we with mirth may safely sing,
    Deo gratias, &c.'

Then they came to the tower of the conduit at Cornhill, and it was decked with crimson cloth like a tent, and on it were the arms of St. George, St. Edmund, and St. Edward, with the arms of England; and beneath were written the words, 'Because the king hopeth in the Lord, and in the mercy of the Most

High, he shall not be moved.' And as the King passed by there came out of the tent a company of prophets, hoary with age, clad in gold, and with hoods of crimson and gold; and they set free a number of sparrows and little birds, who flew about the King, some resting on his breast and shoulders. And the prophets, bowing down before the King, began to sing the psalm, 'Sing unto the Lord a new song. Hallelujah.'

And as they rode to the entrance of the street of Chepe there were men wearing the names of the twelve apostles, and of the twelve kings of England, martyrs, and confessors, who chanted melodious songs as the King passed by. And they sent him wafers of bread and wine from the conduit, that they might receive him as Melchisedek received Abraham when he returned from the slaughter of the kings.

When they came to the cross of Chepe, the cross could not be seen, for there was built round it a fair castle, with columns and arches covering the street, under which the people rode. And on it was built a place convenient for seeing, covered with tapestry; and into it came from the castle a company of fair maidens, clad in white, singing, as they did of old to David returning from the slaughter of Goliath, with timbrel and dance; and they sang, 'Welcome, Henry the Fifth, king of England and of France,' while from the top to the bottom of the castle were to be seen innumerable little boys like angels, dressed in white, casting down upon our King coins of gold and boughs of laurel, while they sang *Te Deum laudamus.*

Then, as they passed round to St. Paul's, there were a number of little pavilions, and in each pavilion, like a statue, stood a fair maiden, with cups of gold in their hands; and as the King passed by they blew out of their cups leaves of gold upon his head. And above was a canopy like the sky, with clouds ingeniously wrought, and above an archangel in bright gold, and beneath the image of the sun, sending forth bright rays, with angels singing around. And there was written upon it, '*Deo gratias!*'

Moreover, the crowd in the streets was so great that the horsemen could scarce ride through them, and from every window and crevice were people gazing; and there were all the most noble ladies and honourable men in the kingdom gathered together, gaily clad in cloth of gold and crimson and bright apparel. And the King, clad in purple, without pride or arrogance, rode gravely, with few attendants, through the praises of the people, the dukes and earls, his prisoners, following him. And it might be seen, from his grave demeanour, that he gave the praise to God alone. Thus he came to the church of St. Paul's, and there offered, and thence passed to his palace of Westminster.

CHAPTER XIV.

THE SIEGE OF ROUEN.

As men have made romances of the sieges and battles and great deeds that have been done in old time, so now I have taken upon me to tell how our liege King Harry the Fifth laid siege, with great array, to the rich city of Rouen, and ended it according to his will. There hath been no greater siege since Troy and Jerusalem were taken. And I may tell it better than another, for I lay there with my liege, and I took right good notice of everything, as far as I was able.

Now, after Pont de l'Arche was won, and the passage of the Seine was forced, the noble lord, the Duke of Exeter, was sent by our King to Rouen, and heralds with him, to the city, to see if they would yield, and also to reconnoitre the ground round about the city, and see how they might best lay siege to it, if they would not obey our liege. And when that renowned duke came before the town he displayed his banners and sent heralds to the city, and warned them, upon pain of death, that they must not withstand our King in his right, but must deliver up the city. Also he did them to wit how the King would go no further till he had it; but before he went from the place, by God's grace he would win it. To this the Frenchmen gave no answer, but bade them go their way, and signed to us that we should stay no longer. Their guns burst forth upon us fiercely and pitilessly, and out came knights on horseback in bright armour keen for battle; and the Duke mustered his men again, and many were taken and slain. When this was done, without delay he rode back to Pont de l'Arche, and told the King of the city, and how it stood.

And now I will tell you of a right cursed deed that the Frenchmen did there before our King came to them, for all the suburbs of that fair town, the churches and houses, they pulled down, for they came out by the gate of St. Hilary and pulled down a parish church—St. Hilary it was called, for the gate was named after it; and by the Caux gate they pulled down the church of St. Andrew, and an abbey of St. Gervais; and at the gate of the Bridge they threw down a church of our sweet Lady, and another of the meek maid St. Katherine and St. Saviour. St. Matthew's they pulled down, leaving neither stick nor stone standing, and a fine church of St. Michel at Martinville, and another of St. Paul a little way off. The hedges or their gardens and their trees they carried home, and burnt the bushes and briers, and made it as bare as my hand. But the gay city was well prepared for defence, and the walls were strong and the ditches deep and defensible. The dyke that was along outside the wall was deep and full wide. The trench was made with a deep descent to defend the ditch, so that no one could come near without danger of death, for no one who fell into the trench could get out again unharmed; and all along the ditch there were pitfalls, and every pitfall was a spear in height, so that no man should be able to stand to fight in them, and so they might know that there were no enemies about them. From the pitfalls up to the wall was a great height. Also it was as full of caltrops as a net is of meshes, and within the town before the wall it was counterwalled with earth so thick and broad that a cart might go along it. This they ordered that the guns might do them no mischief, and they had besides many other contrivances. The city had but five gates, but there were many a score of towers about it, and between each tower there was but the space of six rods, and in every tower lay three guns to shoot diverse ways; and in the wall between each tower all round that fair city there was laid low a strong 'fowler,' with the earth for it to throw; and between every tower were eight small guns to shoot often, and at every ward was set an engine or else a trebuchet, and at some wards there were set more. St. Hilary was one of those. Thus they made their preparation for huge and strong defence.

The Friday before Lammas Day King Harry came before the proud city in rich array, and took up his lodging beside it. On the Saturday he assigned to the chieftains their places round the city, and on Monday he caused it to be proclaimed that every man should take up his position. At the east end of the city, in a house of the Chartreux, was lodged the King with many lords. At the end, to the west, the Duke of Clarence took up his position before an abbey that had been pulled down and sore injured near to the gate of Caux. There he kept in the Frenchmen with great power, and won worship and great honour.

At the other side Exeter, that bold knight, lay at the gate Beauvicine, where, as the Frenchmen came out every day, he beat them back manfully, and won him worship, as he was wont. Between him and Clarence lay the Earl Marshal, next the castle gate, and kept it both early and late; and next him, when he came from Domfront, lodged Talbot and Lord Harington, and when he was dead Sir William of Harington took his retinue. The Earl of Ormond, with a fair train of knights, lay next by Clarence, and that comely knight, Cornwall, was with Clarence always, and many other knights whom I cannot number. Between Exeter and the King lay the Lords Ros and Willoughby, and with them Lord Fitz-Hugh, who was held to be a good and true knight, and Sir William Porter before the gate of St. Hilary, where the war was fiercest, and ever as they came out of the gate he drove them in again with might and main, and won great worship and praise. And until St. Katherine's was yielded up, the bold Earl of Montaigne lay between the town and the abbey, and did much mischief to the Frenchmen. The Earl of Salisbury lay on the other side, and also a comely knight, Sir John de Gray. On Mount St. Michel he lay between the abbey and the town, and Sir Philip Leche between the abbey and the Seine, and kept ward under the hill. Carew, that bold baron, kept ward by the water with a worthy squire, Janyco, above him. On the other side of the Seine lay Huntingdon, warring manfully and winning much worship; and with him lay Nevill and Umfraville and Sir Richard Arundel, and the Lord Ferrars at the gate of the bridge, winning worship every day.

Our King had a great chain made, and fastened by strong piles across the river below the bridge, so that no ships should pass that way; and over the chain he made a bridge, that both man and horse might cross hastily, if need were. And when Warwick was come from Domfront to the King, our liege commanded him to go to Caudebec and lay siege to it. But when he came before the town they began to treat at once, and a composition was granted that they should do as Rouen did, and sealed with this condition, that our ships should pass the Seine with their freight without let or hindrance. So our ships passed up and cast anchor full near to Rouen, as thick in the Seine as they might stand; and so it was besieged by land and water. And when Warwick had ended that he rode to Rouen and took up his lodging between St. Katherine's and the King, until by God's grace the abbey was yielded; and then he lay before the gate of Martinville, where the war was fierce, and manfully repelled their sorties. And when Gloucester was

whē Erle Richard was atte sege of Rōn, there set
first betwēn the kinge tent and seynt
katyns, And whān Seynt katyns was
wonne he was sette to kepe Port chartehule

come from the siege of Cherbourg he lodged before the gate St. Hilary, dreading no peril of stones or quarrels, but lay much nearer the enemy than any other lord by forty roods and more. The Earl of Suffolk and Abergavenny, that comely knight, lay with Gloucester.

Now the Prior of Kilmainham was by this time come to the mouth of the Seine, and landed at Harfleur with fifteen hundred fighting men. They were well arrayed for the war, after the fashion of their country. He hied to the siege full fast, and was welcomed by our liege. But a rumour was spread that the French King, with the Burgundians, would come down by the open plain upon the north side of our host, so the King assigned the Prior and his men to lodge by the wood and keep the highway; and they lodged under the wood and made good their watch and ordinance. Three leagues outside the army was his charge, and the knight gave speedy assent and prepared to receive the first brunt of the attack. Thus our siege was set all round that fair city.

And now I will tell you of the captains of the city. Monsieur Guy le Bouteiller was the chief captain both of the castle and the town, a man of great renown; Monsieur de Termagon was captain of the Gate of Caux, and Monsieur de Roche of the Gate of Beauvicine, with Monsieur Antony for his lieutenant; Henri de Chauffour was captain of the Gate of the Bridge of Seine; John de Matryvers of the Gate of the Castle, and Monsieur Peneux of the Gate St.

Hilary, and the Bastard of Thian at the Gate of Martinville. Graunde Jakes was captain of all the sorties and skirmishes without the city. Each of these captains had five thousand men and more to lead; but of the commonalty there were many thousand men arrayed beside. When our siege first began, those within the city were numbered at four hundred thousand men, women, and children,—a proud store of people for a king to lay siege to. And they were as proud men as ever I saw, skilled in many points of war, and bold in deed, both on foot and horseback. And when they would make an attack they did not come out in one party, but at two gates, or at three, or at all at once suddenly, and at each place there would be ten thousand, royally arrayed, and ready, and daring. It was very pleasant to lead them, but to encounter them was terrible, for much of the war came from the wall, and I never saw greater injury done by shot of guns and quarrels. And when they came out and made an affray there would be shot from at least a hundred guns in the space of an hour, and the quarrels in a little space no tongue could number. And other times they would ride out into the field with shield and spear. Then our King had a ditch made and set full of sharp-pointed stakes, with a prickly hedge all round the city. Sir Robert Bapthorp was comptroller under our King, and he arranged the hedge and ditch. And afterwards they would come out on foot, for on horse it was no longer possible. Our men met them ever on water or land; but many of our men were slain by running too near the walls, and nothing but God's grace could bring them back alive from the thick rain of shot and quarrels, trebuchets, espringales, and other engines, which wrought our men much harm,—especially to Gloucester, for he was lodged so near.

Tidings came again and again that the Burgundians were coming to rescue them, which made the bells ring out full shrill in the city; but they rang not at all after the siege was set until it was taken. But when the tidings reached us that they were close upon us our King said, 'Now, fellows, let every one be merry, for we shall have some fighting soon.' But the news came that they were gone back to Paris. Then again, within a few days, it was said they were at Ponthoise, and that there were of them four hundred thousand fighting men following the Duke; upon which our King commanded it to be proclaimed that every man should lie down in his armour, and outside the camp was made a great ditch, in which were fixed stakes and sharp pikes to wound the horses, and guns were carried and fixed ready to receive an attack. All this work was overlooked by the comptroller; a worthy knight he was, and a busy. Then came tidings they were within twenty miles, and on Thursday it was said they would certainly come on Friday, and the story reached the city. Thereupon our King bade the Earl of Huntingdon try a stratagem. He prepared a company armed with bows, marshalled with their backs to the town, and out of the wood came another company with banners bearing the Burgundian arms; and the two companies fought together, and they cried for succour from the town to come out to them, but they durst not, for they feared it was a trick, and that they would be slain.

But the war went on with sorties and assaults, and the city waited for help from Burgundy until it drew towards Christmas, and bread and drink began to fail in the city. They had nothing but water and vinegar to drink; the bread was nearly gone, and meat, save horseflesh, they had none. They ate also cats and dogs, and rats and mice; and a quarter of a horse, fat or lean, was worth one hundred shillings, and a horse's head half a pound. A dog sold for ten shillings, and a cat for two nobles, while a rat cost forty pence and a mouse sixpence, though there were but few left in any house. A piece of bread, half as big as the hand, was worth a franc of that country, and it was made neither of wheat-meal nor oats, but of bran; leeks and onions sold at a shilling, and glad was a man to get them; an egg at ninepence, and an apple at tenpence. And in the market might be found many a careful heart, not bent on making good bargains, but sad for lack of food, and driven to eat roots and bark and any grass they could find. Then they began to die in that rich city, and they died so fast every day that they were left unburied. Now where once had been pride and joy, with feasting and song, could be heard sorrow and sore weeping, hunger and wailing. Love and kindness fled away; children would give nothing to their mothers, and mothers hid the bread from their children and ate it in secret: so did hunger prove stronger than love.

Still they made a brave show on the walls, that our men might not find out their state; and though many of them stole out of the town, and when they were taken by our watch told us of their misery, we did not believe them, because the defence was still so stout. But in a little space, out of every gate they drove hundreds of poor people. It was a pitiful sight to see women with their children in their arms and old men, making a doleful wailing, and on their knees crying to us, 'Have mercy on us, ye English men!' Our men gave them some of their bread, and we did them no harm, but made them go back again to the ditch, lest they should see the secrets of our watch. Many said they had as lief be slain as go back to the city, and there rose up from them a loud murmur of curses, deep and bitter, against their own nation; and in truth it was full great a sin, for many died there of cold, it being now Christmas time. But on Christmas Day our King sent into Rouen his heralds in rich array, and bade them proclaim to all within the city, and without, that because of the high feast he would provide with meat and drink all that lacked victuals, and give them safe-conduct to come and go. They answered lightly, 'Gramercy!' as if they set little price by it; and to the poor people whom they had put out, they would scarce grant leave that two priests and three servants should bring them food, and swore, 'If any more came to their help they should be shot.'

The poor people were set all in a row, and the priests came and brought them meat. They ate and drank full fair, and as they sat eating so they talked among themselves. 'The Englishman is tender of heart,' they said; 'for see this excellent King whom we have been withstanding, and would never obey nor do homage to him, and yet he hath more compassion on us than our own countrymen; and therefore, Lord Jesus, full of mercy, grant him grace to win his right.'

But when they had eaten and gone their way the truce was at an end, and war took his way. Watch and ward was kept close to keep them in day and night. But hunger broke the hard stone wall, and the captains of the city, the mayor, burgesses, and yeomanry, took counsel together to treat. And on the night of New-year's Eve from every gate a knight called, but no man heard save on Huntingdon's side, at the gate of the Bridge of Seine. A knight asked them what they would have, and they answered, 'We would have a knight of our lineage, or else some baron.' 'Forsooth,' he said, 'I am a knight;' and then they asked what his name was. 'My name,' he said, 'is Umfraville.' Then they thanked God, 'for ye are come of the old blood of Normandy, help us now with your worthy King.' He answered, 'What is your will?' They said, 'We have been at every gate, and have called many times; first for the excellent Lord Clarence, then for the good Lord Gloucester.

Often we called, and waited long; and then to the gate where Exeter lies, but there was none that would hear us. And for Warwick we called more than three times, and for the Earl Marshal. And now help us, and pray all these lords, for God's sake, Who made heaven and earth, and all things, and because they are dukes of great dignity and chieftains of chivalry, they will pray for us to the King, that we may find him gracious. And we beg that we may go to your King ourselves, and beseech him for his knighthood and his princeliness (for he is an emperor, a royal king, and a conqueror), that he would grant us life and his great grace; and that, notwithstanding our offence, twelve of us may come into his presence, for we will tell him that will give him great pleasure.' Quoth Umfraville, 'I will assent.' And he went unto the Duke of Clarence and told him all the matter. And he answered that with right good will he would speak for them to the King; for he was a commendable prince, manful while war did last and merciful when it was over. We find few such lords now. He lacked nothing a lord should have.

And Umfraville took his leave and went forth on his message to Gloucester and the Duke of Exeter, and they thanked God and said they would help to make a good end of it. And Umfraville went to the earls and the lords, and they all said the same to him. God of His great grace show mercy to these chieftains of chivalry, who so soon fell in charity.

Then, on New-year's Day in the morning, Sir Gilbert Umfraville came to the King, and told him all the matter, and prayed for the city. And the King, of his own will and by good advice, granted the city her will, and said, 'Let twelve of them come to me.' And for the King thus showed them mercy when they had so greatly grieved him, and lost him many of his people, and put him to so great cost, he proved himself a right merciful prince and God's own child, for he did good in return for evil.

And when the King had granted, as I have told, 'My liege,' said Umfraville, 'when shall it be?' 'To-morrow,' said the King, 'let me see them.' So Umfraville took his leave and went to the city, and when he was come to the gate he found the estates of the city gathered together thereat; to whom he said, 'I have been with our King, and he has granted your request. To-morrow betimes twelve of you shall go to him, and I will counsel you how ye shall do, for I wot that to-morrow ye shall see the royallest prince of Christendom. Ye never spake with such a prince ere now, nor so soon will again. Think well before ye speak, lest your words be too long; speak but few words and set them well, for a word out of place may bring you all into a bad case. So say nothing without good advice.' They thanked him courteously for his good counsel, and he said adieu, and went his way.

This was Sunday and New-year's Day; and the next day at prime, Sir Gilbert Umfraville, with some of the King's squires, and some yeomen of the crown, went to St. Hilary's Gate. And there came out to them twelve men—four knights, four clerks, and four burgesses, wise men, all clothed in black. And when they came to the house of the Chartreux, the King was at mass, and they waited within the house of the Chartreux until mass was over. Then the King came forth as he had kneeled in his closet, with so high a look and lordly a cheer, and so solemn and grave a semblance, that all men rejoiced to see him. And when the Frenchmen saw him they fell upon their knee, and with meek language held out to him a writing. The King bade Exeter take it, and turned somewhat towards them. In it they besought him, for God's sake, Who made heaven and earth, and all things east and west, and north and south, that he would let them speak to him by word of mouth.

The King bade them 'Say on;' and they were glad, and said, 'We beseech you, for His love Who died on Good Friday, and for His mother dear, listen to us now for charity. Have pity on the poor people who lie in the ditches, and die for lack of bread, and give them leave to go hence.'

The King stood still with grave countenance, and neither did laugh nor smile, but with a lordly presence, neither too mild nor too strange, and gave answer to them. 'Into the ditch of the city I put them not, and that ye know. They were not put there at my ordinance; neither will I suffer them to pass my lines. And as to you, ye know right well ye have kept me from my own city, which is my heritage, when ye should have been my true liegemen.'

And they answered and said, 'As for this city, which we defend, we have a charge from our sovereign liege to keep it from assault, and we are his liegemen, born and sworn to him; and we have also had a strong charge from the Duke of Burgundy: but if ye will grant us our lives and time, that some of us may go and tell our King of our misery, and excuse us of our faith, we will yield up our city, and many of us will become your liegemen.'

To this the King answered, 'Know well, I will not go without my city; and as touching your French liege, he knows, and the Duke of Burgundy too, that I am besieging you; for all the while I have been here messengers have gone between us, and if they like to meet me, they know well they can find me here. And neither for friend nor foe will I go hence without my right. Therefore to send such a message to them now would be no news to them and superfluous for us. There is no need; I will send no such message.'

So when the King had given this answer, they spake no more of that matter; but a knight said it would be fair to win Rouen.

'Rouen,' said the King, 'is my own land, and I will have it whoever withstands me; and those within shall be rewarded as they deserve.'

At that word they were afraid, and a clerk began to speak. 'My Sovereign Lord, it is written in history how that two chieftains had set a day, and were met with their armies, and were arrayed in the field ready for battle. But the weaker party brought to the bigger bread and wine, in token that they should show mercy and pity; and now we bring you bread and wine—even the fair city of Rouen.'

'Rouen,' said the King, 'is my heritage; and from this time I counsel you to do so that ye may find favour; and I grant you now a truce, and if ye will, ye may have grace.'

Then they said, 'Sir, for charity, what will ye do for our poor people who are lying in the ditches and dying like swine? Have some pity upon them, and let them go home.'

To which the King answered, 'I will take advice thereof, and as God shall put it into my heart so will I have pity upon them.' And with that he said adieu, and went his way.

Then these Frenchmen went back to the city with Sir Gilbert Umfraville, and as they went they talked of our noble King. 'In our judgment,' they said, 'he is the wisest of all earthly kings. By his princely carriage, his beauty, and his lordly person; by his great discretion and humanity (for he asks nothing but what is right, and is merciful even in war), he is a worthy conqueror. He should be held in great honour, for well we wot God loveth him!' Thus the Frenchmen went talking of our King on their way to Rouen, and there they took leave of Umfraville, and returned into the city.

On the next day, early, the King commanded two tents to be pitched in Gloucester's trench, one for the English and the other for the French, so that they might keep dry, however great the storms were. And as soon as the pavilions were ready they began to treat with all their might—the wise Earl Warwick and the true Earl Salisbury, with Lord Fitz-Hugh, and the King's steward Hungerford, with others whom I cannot name; and from that city came twelve Frenchmen that were counted discreet. It was a solemn sight to behold—the rich in their array and the people on the walls. The King's heralds and pursuivants in coats-of-arms,—the flower of France, the beast of England, and the castle and tower of Portugal, and the coats-of-arms of each lord in his degree, the gold of them shining as the sun fell on them, while full near was a sight of sorrow and pain. For the poor people that had been put out had scarce a clout on their backs to keep them from the weather, and all that time the rain fell much. There you might see a child of two or three years going about begging his bread, for both father and mother lay dead. The water stood all about, and they lay on the ground crying for food: some starved to death, some mere skin and bone; here a woman holding in her arms a child cold and dead, and there a living babe in a dead woman's lap. And between two dead men you might have found one alive; and they had died silently, without noise or cry, as if they fell asleep, so that he knew not of it. These were sights of difference—one of joy and one of suffering, as if heaven and earth had parted, one for weal and the other for woe.

But let us leave these people and talk of the treaty. We asked much and they offered little; so, though they treated for a fortnight, they could not agree, and they broke up and the tents were pulled down. But the Frenchmen bethought themselves that they had wrought to themselves ill, and as they took their leave they prayed our lords, 'For the love of God continue the truce till midnight!' And the English lords assented, and went their way to the King, and told him how the matter stood.

But in the town it was soon heard how the treaty was broken off, and the poor people rose against the rich, and came upon them with shouts and clamours. 'Ye false churls! ye murderers and man-killers! will ye have no regard to us, who are suffering here, and dying every day? Ye will have to answer before that Judge Who suffered on Calvary, and bought us with His precious blood. If ye would submit to our liege lord he would soon raise the siege. But for your goods, and your pomp, and your pride, ye will not yield to our King, but would rather we should perish by hunger. But if ye withstand we will kill you, and he shall come into his right.' To this they answered cunningly, 'that it was but a feint, that they might make the King ask for less money.' Then they assembled all the city, and every man agreed that there was no way but two—to deliver up the city or to die.

So they went to the gate of St. Hilary, and

called aloud, and a knight named Sir John Robsart answered them, and they said, 'We beseech you, for charity and the honour of chivalry, that ye will speak for us to the Duke of Gloucester, that he may pray the King to let us treat again. We will yield us to his will, our persons and our possessions.' Then the Duke went in haste to the King, and the King granted their request.

Now the Archbishop of Canterbury lay at St. Katherine's, and he went to the King and besought him to give him leave to go to the city and speak with the clergy of it, to bring about a peace. And the King granted him leave, and the pavilions were pitched again in the trench, and the Archbishop set up his between. They treated for four days by day and night, by the light of candles and bright torches, and, by God's grace, they made an end. And, when all was concluded the French prayed that, to save their honour, they might have eight days' grace in which they might send to the French King and the Duke of Burgundy, and tell them how they stood. It was a point of chivalry, and the King granted it willingly. Now the treaty was that, in eight days, if no rescue came, they should deliver up the city and all the burgesses to be English subjects, and pay to our King 50,000*l.*; and, moreover, they should undertake to make a castle for our King on the Seine in three half-years' time. And they were to have their franchise as in old time, and no man might sell within the city but the citizens who dwelt there; and every one in the town who was born a Norman and would not be sworn an Englishman, should be given to the King to punish. And all the soldiers were to lose their goods and lay down their armour, and go out of the town in their doublets, but the King gave every man a gown.

Graunde Jakes was sent to beg for the rescue, and he was glad of the message, and came back no more to Rouen. But he sent a messenger to bid them make an end, for there was no rescue for them that he wot of. So on Thursday, the eighth day, on the feast of St. Wolston, our King sat in royal state in the house of the Chartreux to receive as conqueror the keys of the city. Monsieur Guy le Botellier, with the burgesses of the city, brought the keys to the King, and besought leave to be his liegemen. Our sovereign King commanded the keys to be given to the Duke of Exeter, and made him captain of the city, and charged him to enter in his name and take possession. And the Duke, without delay, took horse and rode forth to the gate that he had lain before so long. With him went many a worthy man, and there was neighing of many a steed and waving of many a banner. And when the gate was opened the trumpeters blew a blast, and the pipes and clarions sounded, and as they entered they shouted with a mighty noise, 'Saint George! Saint George! Our King's right!' The French people were gathered in thousands to see them, and cried them welcome. But, to tell the truth, that people were a pitiful sight; many of them were nothing but very skin and bone, with hollow eyes and sharp visages, but just able to breathe, in colour wan as lead. In every street lay some dead men, and hundreds crying for bread. For long after they died as fast as they could be carried away.

The Duke of Exeter rode first to the castle, and then all through the length and breadth of the city, and set up rich banners in all parts. On the Gate of St. Hilary he set a banner of the Trinity; at the Gate of Caux a banner of Our Lady; and at the Gate of Martinville a banner of St. George. On the castle he set up the arms of France and England.

On Friday, in the morning, came our King into the city, and all the bishops in their robes; and seven abbots with their crosses, with a procession of regulars and seculars with forty-two crosses, came out to meet him, and gave him holy water, and blessed him as he passed. He entered by the wide gate of Caux without pride, without pipe, or blast of trumpet, thanking God Almighty in his heart; and all the people cried, 'Welcome to our lord! Welcome to thine own right!' And with that they cried, 'Nowell!' He rode on a black horse clothed in black damask, with a breastplate of gold, and pendants behind him so long that they hung down on either side to the ground. And those who had never seen him before knew by his look which was he. To the minster he went, and there lighted off his horse. His chaplains met him at the door, and went before him, singing, in response, '*Quis est magnus dominus?*'—'Who is so great a god as our God?' And after he had heard mass and made his offerings he went to the castle, which is a palace of great beauty. There he took up his lodging in great state and splendour. And into the town came fast to the people bread and wine, and fish and flesh. So our gracious liege lord made an end of this great siege.

CHAPTER XV.

JACQUES DE LALAIN, KNIGHT OF THE FLEECE OF GOLD.

How he challenged James Douglas.

Now the good knight Jacques de Lalain, who was continually thinking how to attain to the height of prowess and great renown, labouring with all his might to raise and glorify the house of which he came, and knowing that idleness is the mother of all vice and the destroyer of virtue, thought within himself to send one to the kingdom of Scotland, to carry a letter to James Douglas. In this were contained, as I understand, the articles which Sir Jacques de Lalain was accustomed to send unto all places where he thought to do some deed of arms. Nevertheless, whatever enterprise he would undertake, it was always with the knowledge and permission of his sovereign lord, the Duke of Burgundy, to whom he went and told what it was his intention to do. Now when Duke Philip had heard and well understood the wishes of the young knight, and had seen the letter which he had caused to be written, in order that it might be sent into Scotland, he was very glad, and said, 'God's grace be with you. I see that you desire earnestly the glory and honours of noblesse and worthy renown. Be certain that I will aid you in all your affairs, and go on boldly with what you have undertaken.' Jacques de Lalain thanked the Duke humbly, and showed him the letters which it was his mind to send into Scotland.

There were present his two uncles—to wit, the Lord of Créquy, and Simon de Lalain, lord of Montigny, and many other knights and squires, who praised the letter, saying it was well written. So it was delivered to Charolois herald, who, having received a charge as to what he was to do from Jacques de Lalain, by the leave of the Duke departed and came to Dunkirk, where he took ship, and, with a good wind, in a few days he came to Scotland. There, setting foot on land, he inquired and asked where he should find James Douglas, and he was told by some who knew that he was in a little town where there is a castle named Edin. There he found Earl Douglas, and James his brother. So he saluted the Earl, and gave the letters to James, which were from his lord, Jacques de Lalain.

When James Douglas saw the Charolois herald present the letters to him, he was greatly astonished, desiring to know what was contained in them. He broke the seal and opened them, and read them at length and the articles contained in them. Having read them, James showed them to Earl Douglas and the other barons and knights who were present.

These having read them, they replied and said to Charolois that he was very welcome, and prayed him to have patience, and that he should soon have an answer.

Then James went before the King, who gave him leave and license to do this deed of arms in the manner which was contained in the articles. Thereupon he caused a letter of reply to be drawn up and written, which, being done and sealed with his sign manual, was delivered to Charolois herald, who, when he had taken his leave, with great diligence departed and took ship in a merchant vessel which came to Sluys, where the Duke then was, and with him Jacques de Lalain and his two uncles, the Lord de Créquy and the Lord de Montigny.

When Charolois entered the Duke's court there were many knights and squires desirous to hear his news. The herald went up at once to the Duke's chamber, where at this hour he found the Duke, who had just dined. He saluted him humbly, and then presented his letters to Sir Jacques, who opened them. After they had been read and commented upon, those present began to converse, and it was concluded, by the will and with the leave of the Duke of Burgundy, that Sir Jacques de Lalain should pass over into Scotland to do his deed of arms, which thing he desired above all other.

Whereupon he prepared and arranged everything very honourably, so that no fault could be found with anything. And when he was fully prepared he came to Sluys in Flanders, and took leave of the Duke.

Then he went on board his ship, which was well ordered and furnished with wines and all kinds of victuals, as was fitting. You may be sure he was honourably accompanied by a large number of knights and squires, among whom were his uncle, the Lord of Montigny, and a noble squire, a native of the marches of Bretagne, named Hervé de Mériadecq, squire of the stables to the Duke of Burgundy. These went, not wishing to fight; nevertheless, they did not leave behind them their armour nor weapons, by reason of adventures which they might meet with on the way. They were all richly apparelled, and provided with silver plate and other precious things.

All being ready, about the month of December Jacques de Lalain and those of his company left Sluys, and sailed till they came to the kingdom of Scotland, and to the town of Edinburgh, where at that time were the friends of James Douglas.

Now when Jacques de Lalain and his company were come to Scotland, the Scots of James Douglas's party came to meet him, and there was much talking and many words, for they wished to know why and for what cause De Lalain had sent the challenge to James Douglas; and they were sharp in their questions, and from their manner seemed not very well pleased. But they received for answer that it was not out of hatred, envy, nor any ill-will whatever, but only to do him the greatest honour that Sir Jacques de Lalain had it in his power to show; for that the greatness of his birth, together with the high renown for valour that was in him, made Jacques de Lalain desire his acquaintance more than that of any other knight or lord of the realms of Scotland. Then the Scots of James's party were content.

Now when Sir Jacques de Lalain and James Douglas had spoken together at length of this matter, they agreed to choose each of them two companions, men of birth and of renown. Sir Jacques chose his uncle Simon de Lalain, lord of Montigny, and Hervé de Mériadecq, and James Douglas took to accompany him two noble and puissant lords, the Lord de Halkett and another whose name was also James Douglas, both known as valiant knights.

Of the Lists of Stirling.

The thing being thus concluded, the King of Scotland agreed to be their judge, and fixed the day and place. So the lists were set up at Stirling, and thither the six repaired, to be ready on the appointed day. They were very honourably received by the King, and after the due revels the King appointed the strangers two well-renowned knights, to be with them and aid them with counsel, as is the custom.

When the day came, the King mounted his throne. Jacques de Lalain, Simon his uncle, and Hervé de Mériadecq, entered the lists, all three unarmed, Sir Jacques and his uncle wearing long robes of black velvet furred with marten, and Mériadecq clad in a short robe of black satin furred also with marten. Their harness was borne after them in two chests, covered with the arms of Jacques de Lalain richly embroidered : they were accompanied by the noble friends who had come with them ; and so the three came together to their pavilion and entered in. Then they went to make their reverence to the King, and afterwards returned to their pavilion, where they found their harness ready spread out. There they armed themselves at their ease, and had plenty of time, for their adversaries were more than three hours before they came. Then James Douglas, the Lord de Halkett, and James Douglas, arrived, and came to the entrance of the lists, very nobly accompanied by the Earl of Douglas, and many other lords and knights and their followers, to the number of between four and five thousand men, it is said.

Then the three champions, armed and clad in their coats-of-arms, dismounted and came into their pavilion, and all three together went to make their reverence to the King of Scotland, requesting of him that he would give them the order of knighthood, which thing he liberally granted them. So he descended from his place and made all three knights. Then they entered their pavilion and the King returned to his place. Sir Jacques de Lalain and his companions beheld from their pavilion the three knights returning from the King, each of them clad in his coat-of-arms. They knew them by their arms, and they agreed together that Sir Jacques should fight with Sir James Douglas, Mériadecq with the Lord de Halkett, who was thought to be the strongest, and Simon de Lalain should have to do with the other James Douglas. The challenge was to fight with lance, axe, sword, and dagger, *à outrance*, or at the pleasure of the King; but at the request of the Scots the cast of the lance was forbidden, for they trusted much in their lances. Therefore they agreed together, the uncle, nephew, and Mériadecq, that when they came together against their enemies they would throw away their lances and fight with their axes. According to the rules of the combat, each one might aid his companion, nevertheless Sir Jacques de Lalain said to Mériadecq, 'I believe you will be the first to be rid of your man, yet I pray you, whatever you may see happen to me, that you will neither aid nor succour me in any manner whatever, but that you will leave me to such fortune, good or bad, as it shall please God to send me.' So said they all, and agreed together to do.

So were the three champions arrayed and ready to issue forth from their pavilion, only waiting for the proclamations and ordinances which it is customary to make on a closed field. Very soon these were published duly at the four corners of the lists, the prohibitions being made on the part of the King of Scotland thrice, with sound of trumpets; after which the Lalains and Mériadecq, fully armed and clad in their coats-of-arms, came forth, Jacques de Lalain between his uncle Simon and Mériadecq.

Thereupon the Scots came forth on their side, armed in like manner, Sir James Douglas between his companions. And thus, full haughtily and with proud step, they advanced towards each other, which was a fine thing and pleasant to behold. And as they drew near, seeing that the Lord de Halkett was against Simon de Lalain, Mériadecq would have crossed before Jacques de Lalain in order that he might fight with him, but Simon cried aloud, 'Let each man remain as he is!' So they drew on in this order to fight. And the Lalains and Mériadecq threw their lances behind them, as they had agreed to do, and took their axes and began to fight and rain great blows on the Scots, who defended themselves with their lances.

Sir James Douglas fought with his lance, but soon lost hold of it, and seized his axe and fought a little with that, but not long, for Sir Jacques made him lose that also, as he made him lose his lance. Sir James, being very angry and troubled to see himself thus disarmed of his lance and of his axe, suddenly seized his dagger and thought to strike at Sir Jacques in the face (for he fought without a visor and with his face uncovered), but Jacques, seeing him approach him thus, struck at him with his left hand and made him retire. Nevertheless, Sir James did all he could to strike him on the face. Then Sir Jacques threw away his axe and with his left hand caught Sir James and held him so fast that he could not approach him, and with his right hand he drew his sword, which was a straight blade, and took it near the point, thinking to use it as a dagger, for he had lost his own and knew not how: some said that those who ought to have given it him had not done so. And as he thought thus to use his sword as a dagger and to wound Sir James in the hand in which he held his banner, the blade slipped out of his hand and he was left without arms. And when he saw himself thus disarmed, he quickly and suddenly seized Sir James by both hands, and by strength of arm forced him backwards till he was in front of the King of Scotland, and then twice lifted him off the ground, hoping to overthrow him and put him much out of breath; for Sir James fought with the visor closed, and Lalain had no visor, therefore he could breathe freely: but with Sir James it was not so, as was well seen when the King, having thrown down the bâton, his visor was raised.

We have told how Sir Simon de Lalain met the Lord de Halkett, and how the Lord de Halkett began to fight with his lance, in which he trusted much; but he had it not long, for Sir Simon, who was a skilful knight, strong, and bold, and very expert in arms, soon made him lose it: then they took their axes and struck one another with mighty blows, for they were both tall men, strong in body and limb, and, to look at, knights for worthy deeds; and they showed it that day. The Lord de Halkett was of great strength, and showed it in the heavy blows he heaped upon Sir Simon de Lalain; but Sir Simon knew how to receive them on his axe, and to give in return great and horrible blows when he saw his time: for they were both well-tempered knights, well instructed in the manner of attack.

So they fought a great space, and very valiantly. But after a while the Lord de Halkett, combating with too great haste and ardour, began to grow weary and lose his breath. Then Sir Simon, who was cooler and more wary, seeing that his time was come, began to rouse himself and to strike with edge and point; and he pressed so hard upon the Lord de Halkett that he made him give way and recoil the whole length of the lists. And if the battle had lasted longer, the Lord de Halkett, as every one could see, would have had the worst of it; but the King stopped it.

Now we must speak of the valiant Breton esquire, Hervé de Mériadecq, who that day met and fought with Sir James Douglas, close cousin to the Earl Douglas, and he was a very gentle knight, strong and skilful. The Scotch knight lowered his lance and thought to strike Mériadecq in the face, but he missed and his lance pierced the sleeve of the coat-of-arms on the left shoulder, and leaning his weight on the blow, the lance slipped on the arm and Mériadecq came within reach of him, and with a blow of his axe struck him on the cheek of the bassinet, and bore him to the ground with his face downward, stunned. When Mériadecq saw his adversary on the ground, as it was allowed to help his companions, he looked round, intending to go to their aid if need was; but Sir James Douglas, who was quick and expert, was already on his knees to rise again. So he returned to him, and taking his axe in both hands with the staff of it struck him down again, and he lay stretched on the ground, so that he was in his power if he had wished to destroy him, and he might have done it, for his arms were *à outrance;* but though he saw him on the ground twice he would not touch him, which was nobly done and should be counted to his honour. Then again Mériadecq went to the aid of his companions, who had no need of him; and Sir James Douglas rose quickly to his feet, axe in hand, and Mériadecq returned and they fought together again, and were fighting still when the King threw down his bâton.

But you should know that the gentle squire Mériadecq was one of the strongest and best combatants that could be found, and all the time that they fought together after Sir James rose up again, was greatly to his honour, and he gave him many great blows and drove him backwards at his pleasure.

So the King threw down his bâton, and the guards who were appointed for that purpose took the six champions, and led them to the King of Scotland, and he said that they had all done well and valiantly, and that he held that the arms were accomplished, and it was his will they should be friends together. So each one returned to his lodging. And some days after the King feasted them, and gave them great gifts, for which they returned him thanks. Then Sir Jacques de Lalain and his uncle Sir Simon, and Mériadecq, and those who had come with them, took leave of the King, and departed.

*Of an English Squire who came to Bruges to fight
with Jacques de Lalain.*

And they took ship and came to London in England, but Hervé de Mériadecq took his way through the kingdom of Scotland, and traversed the whole land of England until he came to London, where Sir Jacques de Lalain and his uncle, the Lord of Montigny, had arrived. Now Sir Jacques de Lalain had sent Charolois herald to the King Henry of England, to ask for a safe-conduct for him and his company, and to pray for leave to perform his enterprise at the court of the King of England and in his kingdom. Then Sir Jacques, Sir Simon his uncle, and Hervé de Mériadecq, were in England and in London a long space, but few came to them, neither would the King of England give leave to any of his kingdom to meet Sir Jacques and his companions. So when they saw how poorly they were received, they left London, and put to sea at the port of Gravesend, and the wind being favourable, they came in short time to the port of Sluys, in Flanders, where they tarried a space to refresh themselves. Then they set forth and came to the town of Brussels, where was the Duke Philip of Burgundy, who received them gladly, and made them good cheer, as was their due. And they recounted to him their adventures, and all the princes, counts, barons, knights, and squires, did them honour, and also the Duchess, and all the ladies and damsels of her company.

Then, after the feasts were over, came news to the court of the Duke that there was departed from the kingdom of England a native of that land, by name Thomas, who was coming to the encounter of Sir Jacques de Lalain. The Duke, and the barons of his court, and Sir Jacques de Lalain himself, were much rejoiced when they heard that this English squire had signified his will to accomplish his arms before the Duke according to the manner written in the chapter of arms of Sir James; that is to say, that each one should be armed with such armour as he is wont to wear in the lists, and should fight with axe and sword until one of them should be borne to the ground.

So the English squire came to the town of Bruges, and dismounted at the lodging that they had prepared for him. And Sir Jacques de Lalain, glad at heart, and desiring to do such things that he should be remembered in after times for his high and virtuous deeds, and that all noble knights should take him for an example, prayed leave of the Duke to accomplish his arms against the English squire. And the Duke granted his request, and promised himself to be the judge, and assigned them a day, and caused the lists to be prepared.

When the day assigned arrived the two champions prepared to accomplish their arms, and Sir Jacques de Lalain was the first to enter the lists. Then the Duke, nobly accompanied, mounted the seat which had been prepared for him, and near by were the Duchess of Cleves, the Countess of Etampes, and

THE DUKE OF BURGUNDY

many other great ladies, and in all the galleries and at the windows of the houses round were many strangers. Then soon after, Sir Jacques de Lalain, knowing the Duke to be come, entered the lists, accompanied by knights and squires of the Duke's court, and others with them, and his two uncles, the Lord of Créquy and the Lord of Montigny, called Sir Simon de Lalain. And Sir Jacques passed before the Duke's seat, and made his reverence to him and to the ladies who were there, and passed to his pavilion to arm himself. Soon after entered the English squire, who likewise passed to do his reverence, and then entered his pavilion, he and his men, accompanied by two knights whom the Duke had appointed to counsel him, as had been the custom of long time. When they were armed and ready, and ordinances of the lists were made, and the guards appointed to keep the field, the champions were visited, and they called in question the axe of the English champion, because it was not such as men were wont to bear in the lists; for this axe was made with a blade and a hammer, and a long and broad dagger in front. Sir Jacques de Lalain, by some men of consequence, remonstrated with the Englishman, but he would not for anything give it up, or take one like that of Sir Jacques de Lalain. Then it was told to the Duke, their judge, and he called a council upon it, and it seemed to all of them that the English squire ought to fight with an axe like that of Lalain, but the Englishman prayed urgently that his axe might be left him. When Sir Jacques de Lalain saw that the Englishman prayed so earnestly that he might fight with the axe that he had brought from his land of England, as he said, Sir Jacques, who was courteous and *débonnair* above all men, granted his request; but evil came of it, as you shall hear.

So when they were agreed and the proclamations had been made, Sir Jacques de Lalain came forth of his pavilion, which was rich and fine, and adorned with thirty-two banners of the arms of the lords from whom he was descended by his father and by his mother, which was a fine thing to see, and he was fully armed and clad in his coat-of-arms, with his sallet on his head without gorget or bever, his axe in his hand as his only weapon. Then the Englishman likewise came out of his pavilion, armed in full armour, wearing a great bassinet, with bever and visor closed, clad in his coat-of-arms, his axe in his hand, and girt with a sword; and, eyeing one another, they began to approach, and, beginning to fight, came in front of the Duke's gallery.

Sir Jacques de Lalain, being armed at his ease, and free to get his breath, began to shower great blows on the head of the Englishman, and struck him so often that he made him retire at his pleasure. And to say the truth, the Englishman was doing nothing but consider how best to receive the blows, when Dame Fortune turned against Sir Jacques, for, in giving a blow, he himself struck the point of his adversary's axe, and it touched him between the arm-defences and the gauntlet, and the veins and sinews were cut through, for the axe of the Englishman was marvellously large and sharp.

When Sir Lalain saw himself thus wounded, being strong of will and of high courage, he thought to go on fighting with his axe, but his hand failed him. Then he put the end of his axe under his left arm and fought with the right hand, but could do little thus. Then he haughtily flung his axe on the ground, and quickly seizing the Englishman by the bassinet with his one hand and his left arm, he dragged him to the ground with such force that he fell face downwards with his visor in the sand, so that with a very little knife Sir Jacques could have killed him if he would, but he would not. Then the judge threw down his bâton and the guards came in haste to the Englishman, who was still lying on the ground, and they raised him up and led him to the Duke, where was Sir Jacques, and he said to them, 'Your arms are accomplished, embrace one another, and be brothers and friends.' And they did so, and each one returned to his hostel.

The same day the Duke of Burgundy made a great feast for the English squire, but Sir Jacques de Lalain could not be there for the wound in his arm, which gave him great pain and trouble.

Now by the chapter of arms it was ordained that if Sir Jacques brought to the ground any knight or esquire, the said knight or esquire should be bound to send his gauntlet by an officer of arms wherever he was ordered, but the Englishman replied that he was not bound, for that he was not fallen with all his body to the ground. He said it was very true that his head, and his hands, and legs, were on the ground, but that his body was not, for he supported himself by his hands.

Then Sir Jacques prayed the Duke, who was their judge, that he would decide the question; and it was put before the council, where were assembled the greater part of the notable strangers who had seen the arms,—Germans, Spaniards, Scots, Italians, and others. And it was judged that the English squire had fallen with all his body, and the Duke made known to the Englishman the sentence of the council, and he answered that he was ready to do his *devoir*. But when Sir Jacques saw that the Englishman was judged to have fallen, out of his nobleness and courtesy he acquitted the Englishman of his *devoir* of sending his gauntlet. And he sent to him a very fine and rich diamond, and afterwards he sent him many other gifts, as a fine horse and suit of armour, for which he thanked him much. And the English squire sojourned in the town of Bruges the space of eight days, and was feasted by the court of the Duke and Duchess of Burgundy; and then, having thanked them very humbly, he took his leave and returned to the kingdom of England.

CHAPTER XVI.

OF THE COMING OF MARGARET OF ANJOU, AND OF THE JOUSTS IN THE TIME OF THE TRUCE.

AFTER the truce was made between the kings of France and England and their kingdoms, the French and the English began to have very great intercourse and communication with one another, especially between the merchants and people of divers trades; and also the farmers set themselves to work hard, hoping that by means of this truce a general peace would follow between the uncle and nephew. And, indeed, the truce came at the right time for the English, and for the good cities and fortresses which they held in the duchy of Normandy, for they were in great danger, and were much straitened for want of many kinds of food and other merchandise, especially corn and wine. And in order to furnish themselves, they went in great numbers by land and by water, as well from Rouen as from other towns and fortresses, and even from the open country, to Paris and elsewhere, where they bought great abundance of wine, wheat, barley, and other things which were necessary to them; which goods were then to be had cheap enough in the kingdom of France, and brought them back into their own territory wherever it seemed good to them. And likewise the French went into the duchy of Normandy at their pleasure, to seek and buy whatever they wished and could find there. This commerce went on long and peaceably enough between them, as well on one side as the other.

And at this time, that is to say in the year 1445, by the consent and authority of Charles, king of France, was made the marriage between the King Henry of England, his nephew, and the daughter of the King of Sicily, who was named Margaret, and who was niece to the Queen of France. To make and negotiate these treaties there were employed on the part of the King of England my Lord William de la Pole, earl of Suffolk, Master Adam Moleyns, keeper of the Privy Seal, with other knights and lawyers and persons of good estate. These, when they had finished the treaty for which they had come, retired from Tours, where it had been conducted, and went to Rouen, and thence to England, to appear before their king, to whom they related, in the presence of his council, the state and success of their embassy.

They were very glad of that which they had done, for by means of this alliance they expected to have in France good and powerful friends, especially to help them to attain to a final peace with the King of France, such as might be for their advantage. The ambassadors had agreed with the King of Sicily upon a day when they should return to him, and when he should deliver his daughter over to them at the town of Rouen; and this day they kept as they had promised. And to receive her, King Henry sent to Rouen many lords and ladies richly and splendidly dressed—the Duke of York, the Earl of Suffolk, Sir John Talbot, the Marquis of Salisbury, Lord Clifton, and many lords and knights and squires of great estate. As to the ladies, there were the Countess of Suffolk, Lady Talbot, Lady Salisbury, and others in great numbers. There were also covered carriages and many hackneys, in so rich trappings that few had seen the like come from the realm of England, especially as they entered Rouen, when there may have been as many as fifteen hundred horses, or thereabouts. And in this company there were four hundred archers for the household of the Queen, all dressed alike in gray, and after them came the esquires and the officers; and besides these there were two hundred archers of the body-guard of the King of England, wearing his colours and livery, all richly dressed and wearing on their sleeves a crown of gold. After the knights of the Queen's household came six pages mounted on six hackneys, richly dressed in robes and hoods of black loaded with jewels of silver-gilt. These were all sons of knights. And the first page led in his right hand a hackney, which the King of England sent to the Queen his wife, with a saddle and trappings all of fine gold; and the trappings of the other horses were all of silver-gilt. After these came the chariot sent by the King, which was the most richly ornamented that had come out of England for a long time, for it was covered with a very rich cloth of gold and bore the arms of France and England. This chariot was drawn by six white horses of great price, and was painted within and without with divers colours. In it were the Countess of Suffolk and the Ladies Talbot and Salisbury; and the Countess was in great state, as the Queen would be on her wedding-day. The other ladies followed the chariot according to their rank, mounted on hackneys.

Near the chariot on one side was the Duke of York, and on the other Sir John Talbot, bearing themselves as if the Queen had been in it. The Earl of Suffolk rode on horseback before the chariot, representing the person of the King of England; and after him came thirty-six horses and hackneys with scarlet housings, bearing his coat-of-arms. After the chariot there were also five horses richly adorned, of which two were covered with scarlet velvet and gold, sewn on the inside with gold roses, and the others with crimson damask. And after all these came still another rich chariot, in which were the younger Lady Talbot and other ladies, who were all appointed to go to receive the new Queen of England.

So they entered in this fine and honourable order into the city of Rouen, where much honour was paid them and many diversions given them, both by day and night. Then, certain days after, when the Queen had been received by the aforesaid lords and ladies, they set off together, and went to England, where they were received with great honour, and where there were new rejoicings and fresh pastimes.

During this time, while the truce between the French and English lasted, and the lords and gentlemen had not much occupation in war, the King of France and the other great lords began to give great jousts and other diversions of great expense, in order to keep their men in practice of arms, and also to pass the time more joyously. Amongst others, the Kings of France and of Sicily, at the prayer and by the counsel of the knights and squires around them, allowed many of different kinds to take place in the town of Saumur. In these amusements it seems as if they would follow the rules which formerly the knights of the Table Round are said to have kept, made by the high and mighty prince, the King Arthur. For it was announced by the heralds in several places that there were a certain number of knights and gentlemen who were disposed to hold a passage of arms against all comers, the place being named; in which place were lions, tigers, unicorns, and other like beasts. There were also many other challenges and declarations, very honourable and very haughty. In truth, many feats of arms were performed, and notable assemblies and joyous diversions took place; but by bad luck, on one of these days there was killed by the blow of a lance a gentle knight, a follower of the King of Sicily, named Auvregnas Champion, at which accident all the company was much troubled. Besides, in several of the encounters many were sorely wounded. For this reason the kings and lords began to grow wearied, and abandoned the rest of the undertakings.

But besides these there were held great jousts before the King of France and his princes at Tours, which jousts were arranged, composed, and ordered by a notable and renowned esquire of the King's household, named Louis de Beuil, to meet with an English esquire named Chalon. They were to joust with one another a certain number of courses according to the conditions. Now when the day fixed came, they appeared on the field very well dressed and equipped; and especially Louis de Beuil, who came in great triumph and pomp, accompanied by several great lords, and bringing with him several horses richly dight, and bearing his arms. When they had made their reverence to the King, and all was ready, they ran against one another with great pride and force, several times, and broke their lances; and both of them so well performed their duty that the King was quite content that they should have retired and done no more at that time.

Nevertheless, Louis de Beuil would not consent, and required very earnestly of the King and of his opponent that the feat of arms between them should be finished; which was at length granted him. Thereupon they ran one more course, in which the Englishman struck Louis with his lance through and through below his arm, at the joint of his armour, where he had no crescent or gusset; with which blow he was so grievously wounded that he very shortly after died.

TILTING WITH THE SPEAR

This mishap gave great displeasure and sorrow to the King and to all the nobles who were there, as well as to the ladies and damsels, and not without reason; for, according to the report of those who knew him well, he was one of the most renowned esquires of his party for many and divers good qualities. But since fortune would have it so, the King and his lords paid great honour to Chalon, and assured him against danger to his person. Then, after he had received sundry gifts, he left that place with a safe-conduct, and returned to the country whence he had come, in great sorrow at this adventure which had so unfortunately turned to such great mischance.

CHAPTER XVII.

THE ACT OF ARMS BETWEEN THE LORD SCALES AND THE BASTARD OF BURGUNDY.

The Acts of the full honourable and knightly Arms done between the right noble lord, Sir Anthony Wodeville, Lord Scales, and of Newsells, brother to the most high and excellent Princess, the Queen of England and of France and Lady of Ireland, Challenger, and Sir Anthony the Bastard of Burgundy, Earl of Roche, and Lord of Bever and Beveresse, Defender, before the most Christian and victorious Prince Edward the IV., king of England and France and Lord of Ireland, on the 11th and 12th days of June, in Smithfield.

THE Wednesday next before the solemn feast of Easter, a goodly adventure fell to the noble knight Sir Anthony Wodeville, for, departing from high mass, he betook himself to the presence of his sovereign lady and sister, the Queen of England. And as he was speaking to her on his knees, his cap taken off as his duty was, all the ladies of her court came about, and ere he was aware they tied about his right leg a collar of gold garnished with precious stones, made all of one letter, which in truth was very nigh his heart, and to the collar was tied a noble Flower of Souvenance enamelled. And as he rose all abashed to go to thank them for the great honour they did to him, in his cap, which he had let fall, he found a letter on fine parchment bound with a thread of gold. Thereupon he went forth to the King, his sovereign lord, to tell him his adventure, and to pray his leave to consent to the will of the ladies. Then the King, breaking the thread of gold, found written within as followeth :—

'For the increase of knighthood and recommendation of nobility, and to obey and please my fair lady, I, Anthony Wodeville, Knight, Lord of Scales and of Newsells, Englishman, this 17th day of April, 1465, have received by the ladies the gift of a rich collar of gold, and thereto hanging a noble souvenaunce, which souvenaunce I have taken for emprise, with leave of my sovereign lord the King, to furnish and perform the arms following :—

'I shall be bounden to appear in the noble city of London at the day and hour ordained before the King, against a noble without reproach, who will present himself against me. We shall meet on horseback armed each after his pleasure, with no unfair advantage, and shall run one course with spears. And we shall take sharp swords and shall fight together. I shall furnish the swords and spears, and my fellow shall have the choice.

'The second arms shall be done on foot at the time ordained, and we shall be armed with spears, axes, and daggers, and we shall have but one cast of the spear, and shall fight with the other weapons until such time as one of us be borne down or disarmed.'

Then the noble Sir Anthony Wodeville prayed leave of the King to send to the renowned knight, Sir Antony of Burgundy, that he might come to England and accomplish the arms. And the King, many noble lords standing by, willingly agreed. And he gave command to Chester herald to go forth, clad in the arms of the noble Lord of Scales, and to bear the Flower of Souvenance across the seas to the Knight of Burgundy.

Then the last day of April, Chester entered the town of Brussels, and sent a pursuivant from his lodging unto the Lord Bastard of Burgundy, showing him that he was come out of England with a letter from the Lord Scales. My lord of Burgundy sent two heralds and two pursuivants, who brought him to the Duke's lodging. Then Chester presented his letter, saying, 'Right noble Count, my right honourable lord, Anthony Wodeville, Lord Scales, brother unto the high and mighty princess, the Queen of England and France, recommendeth him to you, and sendeth you this letter.' And the noble lord answered, 'It shall be read, and ye shall be answered as shall content you.' And he went in haste to the Lord of Charolois, and showed him the letter, and they went together to the Duke.

And the morrow after, the first day of May, all the heralds and pursuivants in the court of Burgundy went to Chester's lodging, and brought him to the presence of the Duke on horseback. Then Chester prayed leave to do his errand, and the Duke having given him license, the herald went into another chamber, and put upon him the coat-of-arms of Lord Scales, and bearing on high the emprise in a kerchief, the emprise being fastened in the uppermost border, and covered with the lowest border of the kerchief, he returned into his presence, and making three obeisances as he approached, let fall the lowest border of the kerchief, and stood before the Prince. Then the Duke gave commandment to a lord, a brother of the Golden Fleece, to read the letter of the Lord Scales, the herald holding the emprise on high. And after it was read the Lord Bastard of Burgundy went to the Duke, and asked license to touch the emprise and to accomplish the arms. And thus, coming to the emprise, he said to the herald Chester, 'I pray you recommend me to the Lord Scales, my brother, and thank him right highly for the honour that he doeth to me, and by the license of my Prince I take upon me to touch the emprise;' and with that touching he made a reverent obeisance. Then the Lord Bastard, taking the one part of the kerchief, and Charolois the other, they covered it worthily, and Chester bore away the emprise so touched, and placed it in a chamber apart.

Then Chester tarried there nine days, being worthily entertained with ancient kings of arms and noble heralds, and on the tenth day the Lord Bastard sent him a letter to my Lord Scales. And he sent by his herald Burgundy to the herald Chester the rich gown furred with sables, which he wore at the touching of the emprise, and his doublet of black velvet and the slits of the doublet-sleeves were clasped with clasps of gold and forty guelders. Then Chester took the gifts and arrayed him in the same, and came to court, and gave thanks reverently, and took his leave, and departed, being accompanied for a league out of the town of Brussels by the heralds of the court.

And he returned, and he came to the King at Greenwich on the 23rd of May, and showed to him of his voyage, and how the Lord Antony of Burgundy had touched the emprise. And he bore it to the Lord Scales, and fastened it upon a collar of gold.

Therefore, on Friday, the 29th day of May of the year 1467, the Bastard of Burgundy, with many noble lords, to the number of four hundred, in four carvels, richly apparelled with all manner of habiliments of war, pennons, banners, and streamers, came before Gravesend, about the hour of four in the afternoon, where Garter King-of-Arms had waited for him the space of three weeks. And as soon as he came in sight Garter took and apparelled a barge, and went out two miles to meet him. And he cast anchor before the town that night, and the morning after he set sail towards London. Then a mile or two ere he came to Greenwich there came out to receive

him at Blackwall the Earl of Worcester, constable of
England, with many lords and knights, and aldermen,
and rich commoners of the City of London, in seven
barges and a galley, richly arrayed in cloth of
gold and arras. And he conveyed him forth to
London, and when he cast anchor a little beneath
St. Katherine's he received him into his barges, and
they landed at Billingsgate. And from thence he
was conveyed on horseback by the Constable and
the lords through Cornhill and Chepe, and by
St. Paul's of London to the Bishop of Salisbury's
place in Fleet Street, which had been prepared for
him by order of the King, and richly apparelled with
arras and cloth of gold; and the Bishop's place at
Chelsea, two miles distant, was ordained for him to
try his arms.

The Tuesday next after, the second day of June,
the King came riding from Kingston-upon-Thames
through London, and there went out to meet him
two miles out of town many dukes, earls, and
knights, and the mayor, aldermen, and sheriffs of the
City, and kings-of-arms, and heralds, and pursuivants,
with the sound of clarions, trumpets, and shawms.
The Constable bore the baston on the right hand and
the Earl Marshal on the left, the Lord Scales bearing
the King's sword in the midst. And without the
town the King was met by a procession of the four
orders, and priests, and other religious persons, and
the bishops received him at St. Paul's, and led him
in procession to the high altar, where he offered.
And then he took his horse and rode through Fleet

U

Street, where the Bastard and his fellowship beheld the King. And the Lord Scales turned his horse suddenly and perceived him, which was the first sight and knowledge personally between them. And thence the King went to Westminster.

The same day the Bastard presented himself before the King, desiring the day of battle to be prefixed. Then the King commanded the Sheriffs of London to make barriers in Smithfield, and by the advice of the Constable they were made fourscore and ten yards in length and fourscore in breadth.

And on the Friday came the Lord Scales, in a barge richly apparelled, from Greenwich, where he had tarried long and many a day abiding the coming of the Bastard, and at St. Katherine's, beside the Tower of London, he was received by the Constable and Marshal and the Treasurer of England, with many other lords and knights, and he passed through London on horseback, in a long gown of rich cloth of gold tissue, an herald and a pursuivant bearing his coats-of-arms before him, unto the Bishop of Ely's place in Holborn.

And there was held a chapter at St. Paul's to consider of doubts and ambiguities in the challenge to the Lord Scales, and it was agreed that they should not hurt the horses, but that if the case fell so that a horse were hurt they should be free to take another; neither should they charge with an horse that was terrible to smite or to bite.

Then the Constable commanded the mayor, and

the mayor commanded the sheriffs, to make the lists, and the field was environed with posts seven feet and a half above the ground and three feet in the ground, and between each post bars three inches and a half thick and five inches broad ; and the field was sufficiently sanded. Then the Lord Scales took his horse and came with nobles, and squires, and minstrels, to the east side of the field, and lodged there that night.

The Thursday, the said eleventh day prefixed, the Constable and Marshal provided for the keeping of the field, and they set at every other post a man-at-arms, and at every corner a king-of-arms crowned and an herald, and Garter King-of-Arms and the herald were set on the right hand of the stair of the King's place. And they ordained four men on horseback for the parting of them if the case should so require.

And the field being so arrayed, and the King sitting in his place, with many noble lords about him, and great numbers of nobility and commons assembled about the field, Sir Antony Wodeville, the Lord Scales and Newsells, on horseback, in armour, with nine followers richly attired, came to the bars. Before him were borne two helmets, the one by the high and mighty prince the Duke of Clarence, the King's eldest brother, and the other by the Earl of Arundel ; the Earl of Kent, Lord Harry of Buckingham, Lord Herbert, and Lord Stafford, bearing each one of the weapons, that is to say, the two spears and the two swords.

Then the Constable and the Marshal coming to the bars, asked the cause of his coming. The Lord Scales answered and said, he came to accomplish the arms. Then the King commanded him to enter the field, and he came before the King and did him reverence, and retired to his pavilion. And his own horse was trapped in white cloth of gold, with a cross of St. George of crimson velvet, bordered with a fringe of gold half a foot long. The second horse had trappings of tawny velvet, with many great bells. The third was trapped in russet damask to the foot, and the fourth in purple damask, bordered with blue cloth of gold. The fifth horse was trapped to the foot in blue velvet, with plaits of crimson satin and a border of green velvet and gold. The sixth horse had trappings of crimson cloth of gold furred with sable. The seventh was trapped in green damask to the foot, bordered with russet cloth of gold half a foot broad. The eighth horse had demi-trappings of tawny damask, and the ninth long trappings of ermine, bordered with crimson velvet with tassels of gold. And on every horse rode a page richly attired in mantles of green velvet, embroidered with goldsmiths' work.

And his pavilion was of double blue satin, embroidered with his letters and his motto, and bearing eight banners.

Then there came to the barrier the Bastard on horseback, with seven followers richly attired, and his own horse was harnessed in a rich, goodly fashion of crimson, with silver bells, every other one being gilt.

The second horse was led before him by four knights, and it was covered with trappings bearing his arms. The third horse, following him, had trappings of ermine to the foot, with the reins of fine sable. The fourth horse was covered with cuirbouly (leather), and over it a rich cloth of gold. The fifth had trappings of crimson velvet to the foot, bearing a device of eyes full of tears wrought in gold. The sixth horse was covered to the foot in purple cloth of silver, and the seventh was trapped in green velvet. The eighth horse was trapped in fine sables down to the foot, with the reins of ermine. And his pages were arrayed in gowns of violet colour, with goldsmiths' work.

And he demanded entrance from the porters, and by the King's license came into the field, the Duke of Suffolk bearing his helmet before him, and accompanied by many noblemen. And he came before the King and said, 'Right high, right mighty, and right excellent prince, I am come hither before your presence as my judge to accomplish the act of arms.' And the King gave him leave and license.

Then he departed to his place and put on his helmet. And the swords and spears being brought before the King, he delivered them to the Bastard to have the choice. And when he had chosen, proclamation was made at the four corners of the field that no man should approach the lists, or make any noise or shout, or in any manner aid or trouble the noble knights who were to do their arms within the lists.

Then the Constable commanded an herald to cry, '*Laissez-aller!*' And they ran a course courageously, seeking one another, and both were unhit. Then the Lord Scales threw away his spear, his bever, and the armour of his arms; and the Bastard laid aside his also. But the Lord Scales was sooner ready, and he sought the Bastard and assailed him with a thrust in the neck; and the Bastard struck him an edge-stroke on his helmet. But the Bastard's horse, having armour on his head, struck against the Lord Scales' saddle, and with the blow the Bastard and the horse went to the ground.

Then the Lord Scales, seeing him down, turned about and held up his sword; and seeing he could not rise, rode straight to the King, and alighted, and bade them take the trapper from the horse, showing that his horse had no armour on his head.

Then the King commanded to take up the Bastard; and he came before the King. And whereas it was agreed that if any horse failed, it should be lawful for his master to have another, it was demanded whether he so willed, but he answered that he willed it not. So the King commanded and they went to their lodging.

The morrow after the King came to the field, and Lord Scales, armed all save his bassinet, came to the gate, his horse trapped to the foot in crimson velvet, with his arms embroidered. And there followed him eight coursers in harness of one suit, and upon them eight pages in rich habiliments, the Duke of Clarence bearing his bassinet, and the other lords bearing the weapons — two casting-spears, two axes, and two daggers. The Constable demanding the cause of his coming, he answered as before, and the King gave him license to enter the field. Then having alighted and done his due reverence before the King, he resorted to his pavilion, his banner being held by Clarencieux King-of-Arms before his tent.

And the Bastard came riding to the bars, worshipfully accompanied by many lords, and with the King's license entered the field; and having done his due reverence resorted to his pavilion, being clad in a long gown of blue velvet. And his pavilion was of white and purple damask, the valance of green velvet being embroidered with his motto, '*Null*' *ne cy frete.*'

Then the weapons being presented to the King, he commanded the casting-spears to be laid aside, saying that, inasmuch as it was but an act of pleasure, he would have none such mischievous weapons used before him, but of the daggers and the axes the Bastard should have the choice.

And proclamation having been made as before the Constable visited the Lord Scales in his tent, and found him ready; and then he went to the Lord Bastard in his tent. And the King commanded them to cry, '*Laissez-aller!*' And right as the King-of-Arms made the cry the Lord Scales opened his pavilion, and at the second '*Laissez-aller!*' entered the field, and stood and gave token that he was ready with hand, and foot, and axe; inasmuch as he laid his

axe upon his shoulder, and often changed it from
hand to hand. And then they advanced, and right
before the King assailed each other in such wise that
the Lord Scales, with the point of his axe, struck
through one of the ribs of the Bastard's plate-armour,
as the Bastard showed him after the field. And so
they fought together, the Lord Scales with the head
of his axe before, and the other with the small end,
and smote many great and strong strokes, till at the
last the Lord Scales struck him in the side of the
visor of his bassinet. Then the King, perceiving the
perilous blow, cast his staff, and with high voice cried,
'Whoo!' Notwithstanding, in the parting of them,
there were given two or three great strokes, and one
of the men-at-arms' staves was broken between them,
and they, so parted, were brought up before the
King's grace.

The Lord Scales fought with his visor open,
which was thought jeopardous; the Lord Bastard
fought closed. And so they were brought up
before the King. He commanded them each to
take the other by the hands, and to love each other
as brothers in arms; which they did. And there
they gave each other as courteous, goodly, and
friendly language as could be, and went together
into the midst of the field. And then every man
departed to his lodging.

As for the King of England and the Queen,
they had prepared a supper in the Mercers' Hall,
and I saw there sixty or eighty ladies of such

THE LORD SCALES & THE BASTARD OF BURGUNDY

noble houses that the least of them was the daughter of a baron; and the supper was great and plentiful, and the Bastard and his people feasted gaily.

And the next day Sir Jean de Chassa, and a Gascon squire named Louis de Bretelles, a servant of the Lord Scales, did arms on foot, and accomplished the arms without much injury. And the next day they did arms on horseback, in which Jean de Chassa won great honour, and was accounted a good runner with the lance. And the day after Sir Philippe Bouton did arms against a squire of the King's. This squire was a Gascon named Thomas de la Lande, and he was a fine jouster and a good man. But there arose a question between them, for those who attended Messire Philippe Bouton said that the accoutrements of Thomas de la Lande were too advantageous. Then the King's people went to see, and found it was true, at which the King was not pleased. However, they agreed to finish their arms, and each one to do the best he could, and so the arms were accomplished. Then the Bastard prayed the ladies to dine with him on Sunday, and chiefly the Queen and her sisters, and he made great preparation. But at that time the news came to the Bastard that the Duke of Burgundy was dead; and he mourned greatly when he heard of the death of his father, and all the nobility who were with him. So their pleasures were all turned to weeping and tears. And the Bastard took leave of the King of England, of the Queen, and of the ladies, very sadly. And his preparations were all lost, for he withdrew his proposal of the feast, and returned to Bruges.

London: Printed by STRANGEWAYS & SONS, Tower Street, St. Martin's Lane.

www.ingramcontent.com/pod-product-compliance
Lightning Source LLC
Chambersburg PA
CBHW030002240426
43672CB00007B/796